Editorial Project Manager
Lorin E. Klistoff, M.A.

Managing Editor
Karen J. Goldfluss, M.S. Ed.

Illustrator
Mark Mason

Cover Artist
Brenda DiAntonis

Art Production Manager
Kevin Barnes

Art Coordinator
Renée Christine Yates

Imaging
James Edward Grace

Publisher
Mary D. Smith, M.S. Ed.

Bible Memory Verse Crafts

Author

Mary Tucker

Teacher Created Resources, Inc.
6421 Industry Way
Westminster, CA 92683
www.teachercreated.com
ISBN: 978-1-4206-7062-2
© 2007 Teacher Created Resources, Inc.
Reprinted, 2010
Made in U.S.A.

Table of Contents

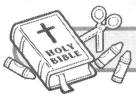

Table of Contents

Table of Contents

Introduction

God tells us over and over again how important it is to study His Word, meditate on it, and apply it to our lives. And of all the things our children memorize, Bible verses are the most important, without a doubt. We are never too young or too old to hide God's Word in our hearts and minds. The Scriptures your children memorize now will be with them to bless them and guide them throughout their lives.

The crafts in this book will help children memorize Bible verses that will teach them about God and what He expects from them. (*Note:* This book uses the *New International Version* of the Bible.) As you go through each craft with them, read the Bible verse together and talk about it to make sure they understand exactly what it means and what God wants to teach them through it. The crafts are simple, but interesting projects made from easily obtainable materials such as cardstock, construction paper, colored markers or crayons, craft sticks, felt, paper plates, foil, glitter, yarn, etc. Clear step-by-step directions are provided for each craft, as well as any reproducible patterns you may need.

Most of the Bible verses are favorite ones which children will encounter in their Sunday School lessons. Some are short while others are longer. However, even the longer verses are easy to memorize if children break them down into phrases. The verses are taken from both the Old and New Testaments. Each Bible verse craft stands on its own and may be used on its own or as a supplementary activity with a Bible story lesson.

As your children learn these verses and create the crafts, they will begin to understand that God wants to communicate with them through His written Word, the Bible. He has provided His Word to guide and encourage them, to show them right from wrong, to teach them about His Son, to tell them about heaven, and to show them how to live for Him every day. Memorizing His Word will draw them closer to God as nothing else can.

"The unfolding of your words gives light; it gives understanding to the simple." (Psalm 119:130) Light up your children's lives by encouraging them to memorize God's Word!

Genesis 1:27

"So God created man in his own image, in the image of God he created him; male and female he created them."

Materials

- patterns (page 7)
- crayons or colored markers
- cardboard tube (1" section)
- cardstock
- scissors
- glue

Directions

1. Copy the patterns on cardstock.

2. Color and cut out the patterns.

3. Glue the patterns of Adam and Eve, back to back, to a 1" section of cardboard tube (from a toilet paper or paper towel roll) at the bottom. (See picture to the right.)

4. Then glue the figures of Adam and Eve together at the top and sides. (See picture.)

5. Stand up the two-sided figure and read the Bible verse, starting on the Adam side.

Finished Product (back)

Finished Product (front)

So God created man in his own image, in the image of God he created him;

Adam Pattern

So God created man in his own image, in
the image of God he created him;

Eve Pattern

male and female he created them.
(Genesis 1:27)

Exodus 33:14

"The Lord replied, 'My Presence will go with you, and I will give you rest.'"

Materials

- patterns (below and page 9)
- crayons or colored markers
- cotton balls
- glue
- cardstock
- scissors
- tape

Directions

1. Copy the patterns on cardstock.

2. Color and cut out the picture.

3. Cut out the cloud patterns and glue cotton on them. (Do not glue cotton on the tabs.)

4. Tape the clouds on top of the cloud shapes on the mountain scene picture. (Tape only the tabs so the clouds can be lifted up.)

5. Lift up the clouds to read the Bible verse about what God will do.

Finished Product

Cloud Patterns

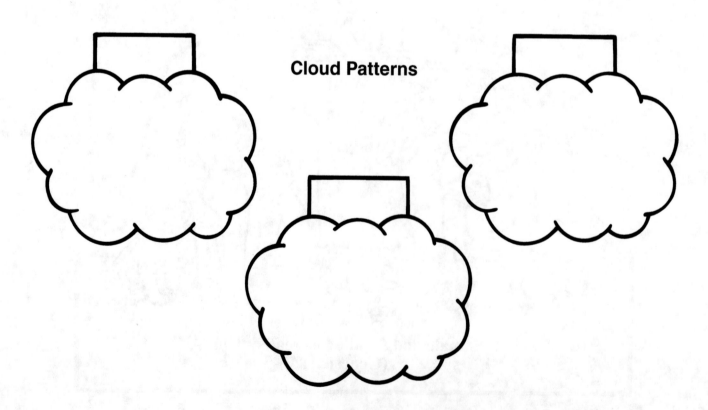

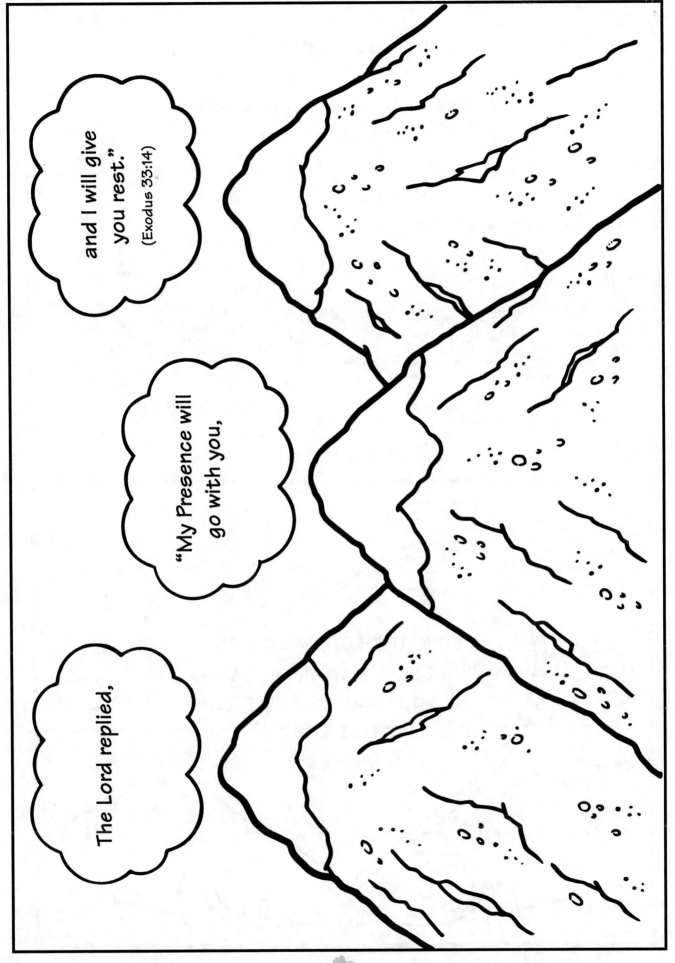

Deuteronomy 6:5

"Love the Lord your God with all your heart and with all your soul and with all your strength."

Materials

- pattern (below)
- crayons or colored markers
- yarn
- cardstock
- scissors
- glue

Directions

1. Copy the pattern on cardstock.

2. Color and cut out the pattern.

3. Spread a line of glue around the hearts and the borders as shown.

4. Place yarn on the glue line and lightly pat it down. Let the glue dry.

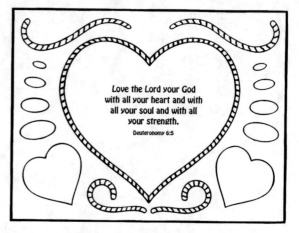

Finished Product

Card Pattern

Deuteronomy 8:6

*"Observe the commands of the Lord your God,
walking in his ways and revering him."*

Materials

- pattern (below)
- crayons or colored markers
- tongue depressor or craft stick
- cardstock
- scissors
- tape or glue

Directions

1. Copy the patterns on cardstock.
2. Color and cut out the patterns.
3. Glue or tape the patterns back to back on the end of a tongue depressor or craft stick.
4. Read the first part of the Bible verse and look at the picture, then turn it over to read the rest of the verse and look at the other picture.

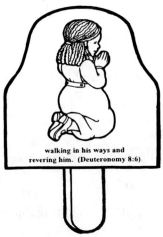

Finished Product

Pattern (Front)

**Observe the commands of the
Lord your God,**

Pattern (Back)

**walking in his ways and
revering him. (Deuteronomy 8:6)**

Joshua 1:8

"Do not let this Book of the Law depart from your mouth; meditate on it day and night, so that you may be careful to do everything written in it. Then you will be prosperous and successful."

Materials

- pattern (below)
- crayons or colored markers
- tape or glue
- cardstock
- scissors

Directions

1. Copy the pattern on cardstock.

2. Color it and cut it out.

3. Tape or glue the tab to the area on the pattern marked with a black dot.

4. Stand up the figure as a reminder to study God's Word and think about it every day.

Finished Product

Pattern

Do not let this Book of the Law depart from your mouth; meditate on it day and night, so that you may be careful to do everything written in it. Then you will be prosperous and successful. (Joshua 1:8)

1 Samuel 16:7b

"'Man looks at the outward appearance, but the Lord looks at the heart.'"

Materials

- patterns (below and on page 14)
- cardboard
- crayons or colored markers
- scissors
- red construction paper
- glue
- aluminum foil

Directions

1. Copy the patterns. Make two copies of the mirror pattern.
2. Trace around the mirror pattern on stiff cardboard and cut out the shape.
3. Trace around the heart pattern on red construction paper and cut it out.
4. Cut out the two parts of the Bible verse.
5. Glue the two mirror patterns on the cardboard mirror shape, one on each side.
6. Cut out a piece of aluminum foil to fit the center space on one side of the mirror. Glue it on the mirror.
7. Glue the red heart to the center of the other side of the mirror.
8. Glue the first part of the Bible verse ("Man looks at the outward appearance,") beneath the mirror with the aluminum foil.
9. Glue the second part of the Bible verse ("but the Lord looks at the heart.") beneath the red heart on the other side of the mirror.

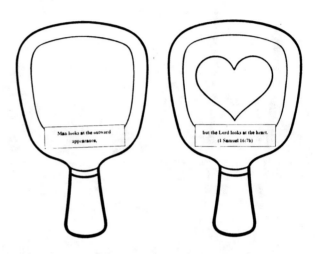

Finished Product

Verse Patterns

"Man looks at the outward appearance,

but the Lord looks at the heart."
(1 Samuel 16:7b)

Heart Pattern

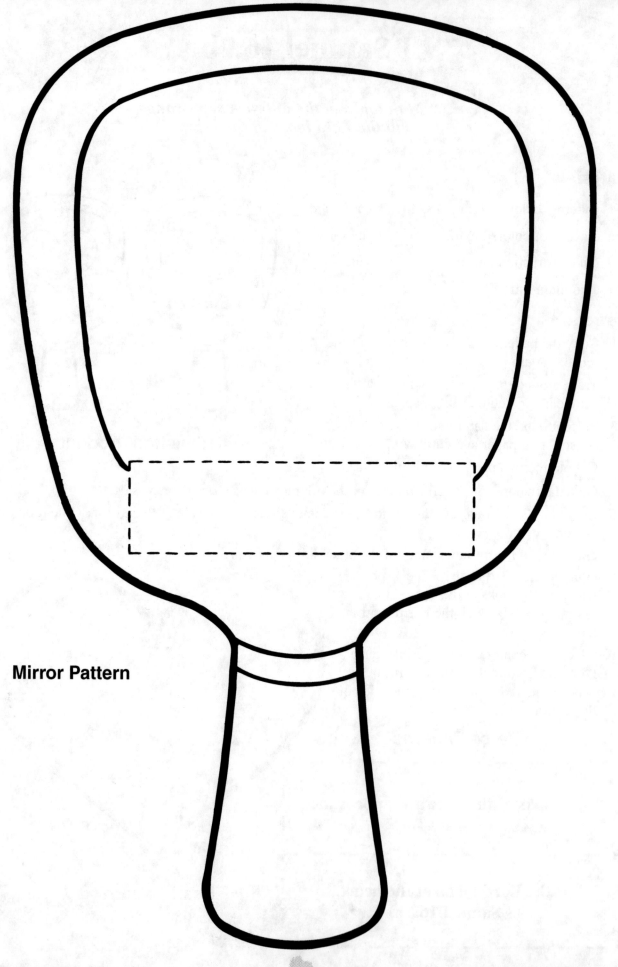

Mirror Pattern

2 Samuel 22:33

"'It is God who arms me with strength and makes my way perfect.'"

Materials

- pattern (below)
- crayons or colored markers
- small brad fasteners
- cardstock
- scissors
- pencil

Directions

1. Copy the patterns on cardstock.
2. Color and cut out the patterns.
3. Connect the arms to the body with brad fasteners, poking holes with the pencil at the shoulders where indicated.
4. Move the figure's arms over his head. Fit the weight in his hands.
5. Thank God for the strength He gives you every day to live for Him.

Finished Product

Weight Pattern

"It is God who arms me with strength and makes my way perfect." (2 Samuel 22:33)

Body Pattern

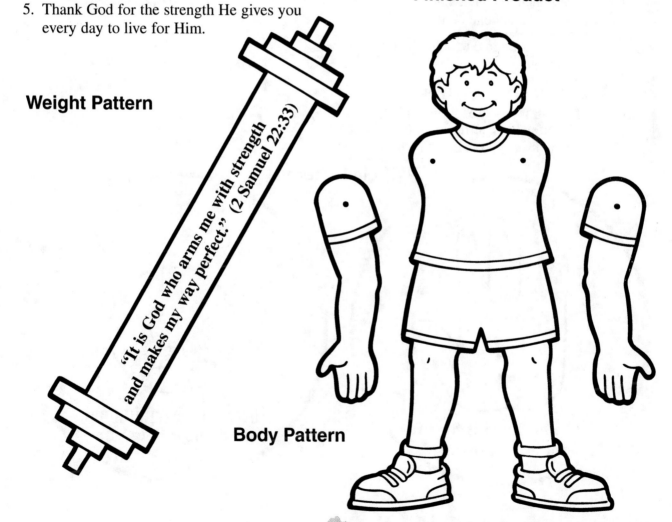

Job 12:10

"'In his hand is the life of every creature and the breath of all mankind.'"

Materials

- patterns (below)
- crayons or colored markers
- string (two 4" pieces)
- hole punch
- cardstock
- scissors
- glue

Directions

1. Copy the circle patterns on cardstock.

2. Color the two circles and cut them out.

3. Glue the circles back to back—one right side up, the other upside down.

4. Use a hole punch to punch a hole on the right side of the circle and one on the left.

5. Tie a piece of string in one hole, then tie a piece of string in the other hole.

6. Hold the circle strings loosely in each hand and twist the string between your thumb and first fingers. Then pull the strings taut to make the circle spin and see who is in God's hand.

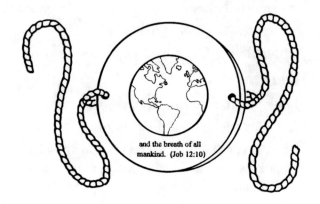

Finished Product

Circle Patterns

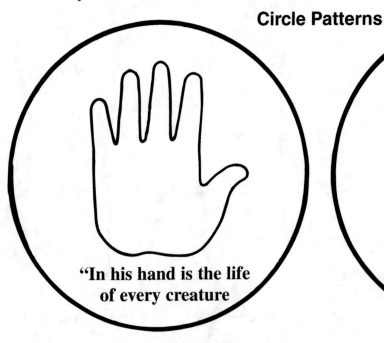

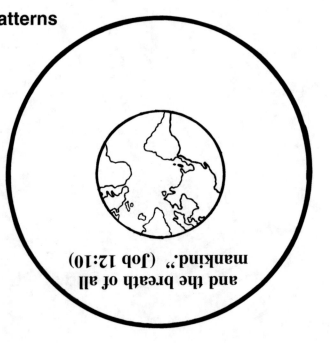

Job 12:13

*"'To God belong wisdom and power;
counsel and understanding are his.'"*

Materials

- pattern (below)
- crayons or colored markers
- dowel rod (or an unsharpened pencil)
- yarn
- white paper
- scissors
- glue or tape

Finished Product

Directions

1. Copy the Bible verse pattern.
2. Color and cut out the pattern.
3. Wrap the pattern around into a circular tube and glue or tape it down.
4. Put a dowel rod (or pencil) through the tube.
5. Tie yarn to both ends of the rod for a hanger.
6. Spin the tube around to read the Bible verse.

Verse Pattern

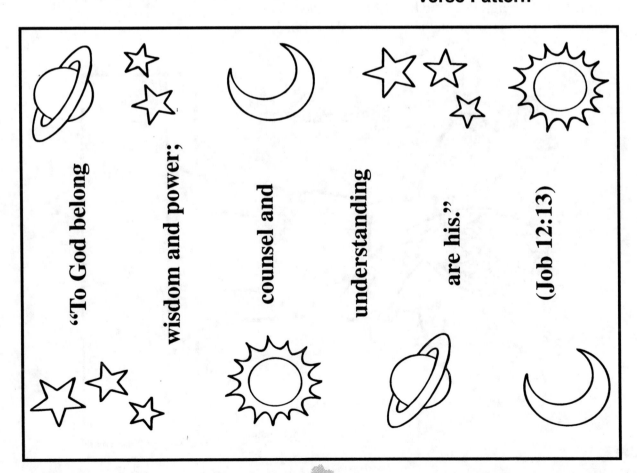

Job 19:25

"'I know that my Redeemer lives, and that in the end
he will stand upon the earth.'"

Materials

- patterns (this page and page 19)
- crayons or colored markers
- tape
- cardstock
- scissors

Directions

1. Copy the patterns on cardstock.
2. Color and cut out the patterns.
3. Fold the earth pattern in half so it stands up.
4. Tape the figure of Jesus to the lower half of the earth pattern. Then fold it down flat.
5. Read the first part of the Bible verse on the top half of the earth. Then fold up the figure of Jesus and read the rest of the verse on the bottom of the earth.

Finished Product

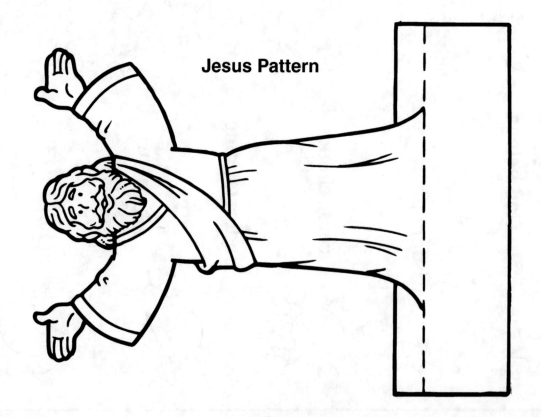

Jesus Pattern

Earth Pattern

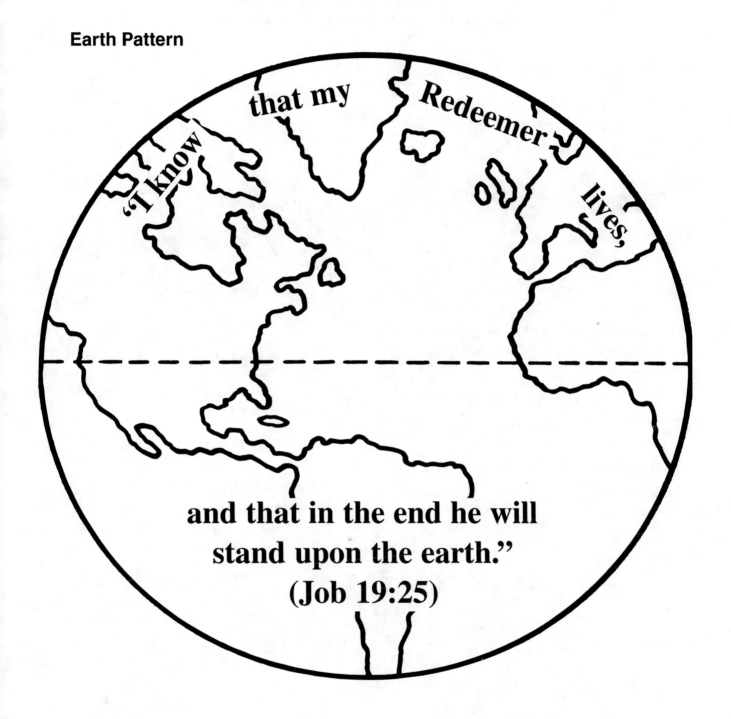

"I know that my Redeemer lives, and that in the end he will stand upon the earth." (Job 19:25)

Job 33:4

"'The Spirit of God has made me;
the breath of the Almighty gives me life.'"

Materials

- pattern (page 21)
- cardstock
- colored markers
- scissors
- balloon

Directions

1. Copy the feet pattern on cardstock.

2. Color and cut out the feet all in one piece. Be sure to cut a slit down the middle.

3. Carefully draw your face on the balloon. (You may prefer to do this after the balloon is blown up.)

4. Blow up the balloon and tie the end closed.

5. Slip the end of the tied balloon in the slit between the feet so it stands up.

6. Read the words on the feet to memorize the Bible verse.

Finished Product

"The Spirit of God has made me;
the breath of the Almighty gives me life."

(Job 33:4)

Psalm 1:1–2

"Blessed is the man who does not walk in the counsel of the wicked or stand in the way of sinners or sit in the seat of mockers. But his delight is in the law of the Lord, and on his law he meditates day and night."

Materials

- pattern (below)
- cardstock
- crayons or colored markers
- scissors

Directions

1. Copy the pattern on cardstock.

2. Color and cut out the pattern.

3. Cut out the two circles as shown. (The teacher will need to do this for younger children.)

4. Bend the figure back slightly at the waist.

5. Put the pointer finger and middle finger in the holes to be the man's legs.

6. Say the Bible verse and act it out with your finger puppet—walking, standing, and sitting as you say those words, then kneeling in prayer for the last few words of the verse.

Finished Product

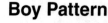

Boy Pattern

22

Psalm 4:8

*"I will lie down and sleep in peace, for you alone,
O Lord, make me dwell in safety."*

Materials

- patterns (below and on page 24)
- paper plate
- crayons or colored markers
- scissors
- glue
- cardstock
- craft stick or tongue depressor
- gold or silver star stickers

Finished Product

Directions

1. Copy the patterns on cardstock.
2. Color and cut out the patterns.
3. Color the top half of the paper plate black or dark blue for a night sky. Add star stickers.
4. Glue the camping scene pattern on the paper plate beneath the "sky" half.
5. Glue the child pattern on the end of a craft stick or tongue depressor.
6. Glue the Bible verse on the plate scene.
7. Cut a slit across the middle of the sleeping bag in the scene.
8. Slide the figure of the child on the stick up through the slit. Move the figure to make the child lie down and sleep as you read the Bible verse.

Sleeping Child Pattern

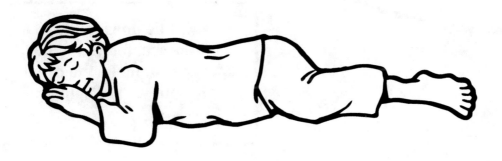

Camping Scene Pattern

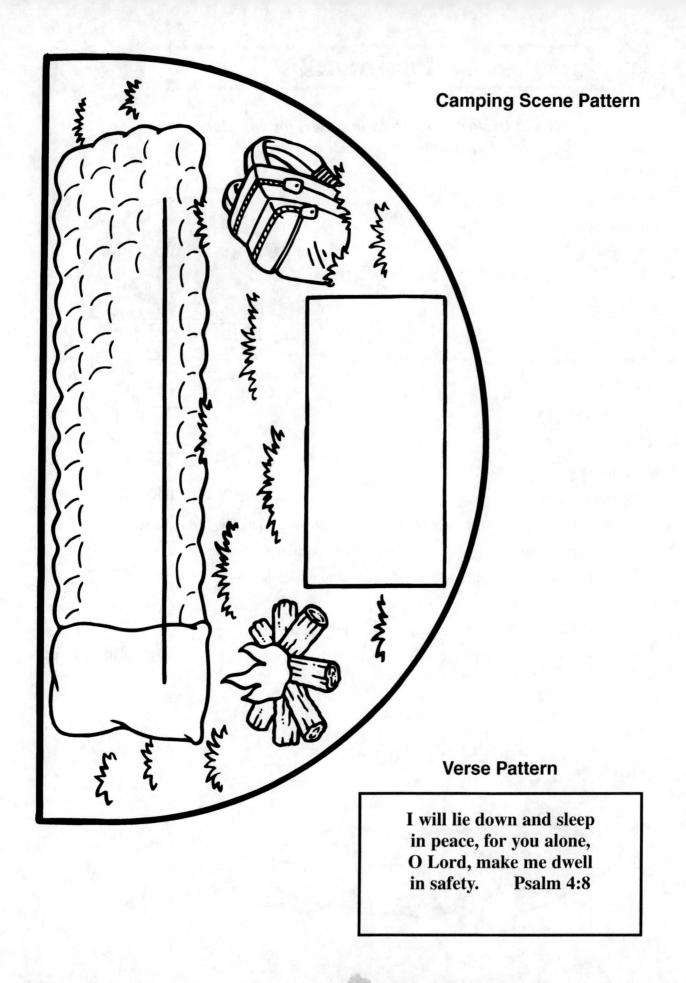

Verse Pattern

I will lie down and sleep
in peace, for you alone,
O Lord, make me dwell
in safety.   Psalm 4:8

Psalm 8:9

"O Lord, our Lord, how majestic is your name in all the earth!"

Materials

- patterns (below)
- crayons or colored markers
- cardstock
- scissors
- glue
- plastic container lid (about 3 1/2" in diameter)
- clear adhesive plastic
- hole punch
- string

Directions

1. Copy the earth patterns on cardstock.
2. Color and cut out the patterns.
3. Glue a pattern on each side of the lid.
4. Cover both sides with clear adhesive plastic.
5. Punch a hole in the top of the lid and tie on a string for a hanger.
6. Hang the Bible verse in a doorway or window.

Finished Product

Earth Patterns

O Lord, our Lord, how majestic is your name in all the earth! (Psalm 8:9)

Psalm 9:2

"I will be glad and rejoice in you; I will sing
praise to your name, O Most High."

Materials

- pattern (below)
- crayons or colored markers
- cardstock
- scissors
- clear adhesive plastic
- pin backing (available in most craft stores)
- glue or masking tape

Directions

1. Copy the musical notes pattern on cardstock.
2. Color and cut out the pattern.
3. Cover the notes, front and back, with clear adhesive plastic to protect them. Trim excess.
4. Glue a pin to the back of the notes and let the glue dry, or roll up a piece of masking tape and stick it to the back of the notes.
5. Attach the notes to your shirt or jacket to let everyone know that you praise God. Memorize the Bible verse so you can tell it to people even when you are not wearing the pin.

Finished Product

I will be glad
and rejoice in you;
I will sing
praise to your name,
O Most High.

(Psalm 9:2)

Musical Notes Pattern

Psalm 9:10

"Those who know your name will trust in you, for you, Lord, have never forsaken those who seek you."

Materials

- patterns (page 28)
- crayons or colored markers
- cardstock
- scissors
- hole punch
- brad fasteners

Directions

1. Copy the patterns on cardstock.

2. Color the patterns and cut them out. (Color the shirt a light color so you can read the Bible verse through the color.)

3. Punch holes at the circles on the body pattern and the legs pattern.

4. Use brad fasteners to connect the legs to the boy's body.

5. Read the Bible verse on the boy's shirt. Make the figure bow on his knees as you read about those who seek the Lord.

6. Memorize the Bible verse so you can say it without looking as you make the boy move.

Finished Product

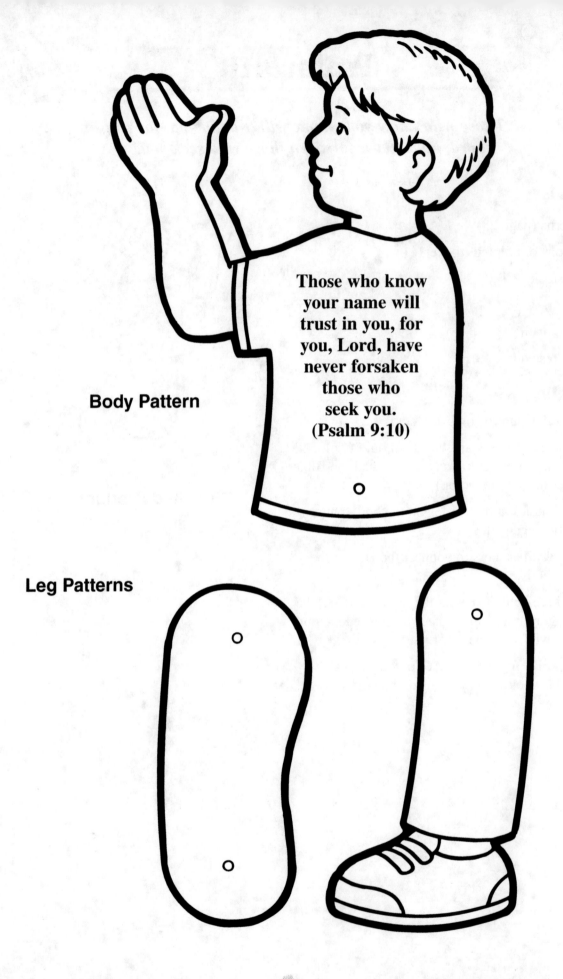

Body Pattern

Those who know
your name will
trust in you, for
you, Lord, have
never forsaken
those who
seek you.
(Psalm 9:10)

Leg Patterns

Psalm 16:11

"You have made known to me the path of life; you will fill me with joy in your presence, with eternal pleasures at your right hand."

Materials

- patterns (this page and page 30)
- colored markers and fabric markers
- fabric or construction paper (light colors, at least 14" square)
- various fabric scraps (felt, taffeta, cordoroy, silk, velour, etc.)
- buttons, rick-rack, ribbon, and other decorative materials
- cardstock
- glue
- scissors
- wooden dowel
- yarn

Directions

1. Copy the patterns and Bible verse on cardstock. Cut them out.
2. Cut a piece of fabric or construction paper in the shape you want for your banner. Cut the bottom edge in a fringe.
3. Fold back the top edge of the banner.
4. Trace around the patterns on fabric scraps of various kinds and cut them out.
5. Glue the Bible verse and fabric pieces on the banner.
6. Glue on buttons and other items to decorate your banner.
7. Glue the folded back top of the banner to a wooden dowel.
8. Attach yarn to both ends of the rod for a hanger.

Body Pattern

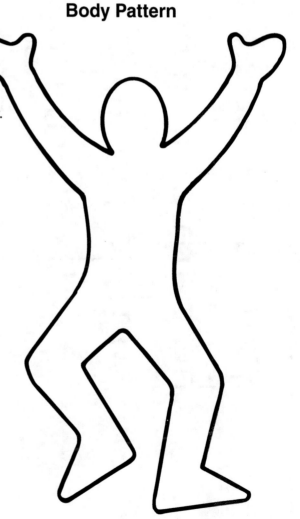

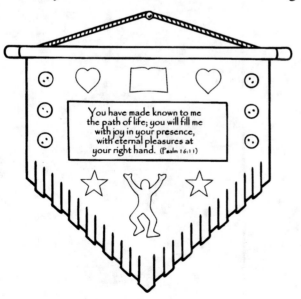

Finished Product

You have made known to me
the path of life; you will fill me
with joy in your presence,
with eternal pleasures
at your right hand.

(Psalm 16:11)

Shapes and Bible Verse Patterns

30

Psalm 18:28

"You, O Lord, keep my lamp burning;
my God turns my darkness into light."

Materials

- pattern (page 32)
- cardstock
- scissors
- tape or glue
- crayons or colored markers
- beige or tan fabric (or string)
- red fabric (or tissue paper)

Directions

1. Copy the pattern on cardstock.
2. Color and cut out the pattern.
3. Cut out a piece of red fabric (or tissue paper) and glue it on the flame.
4. Cut out a piece of beige or tan fabric (or string) and glue it on the lamp's wick.
5. Roll a half sheet of cardstock (about $5\frac{1}{2}$" x $8\frac{1}{2}$") into a tube and glue or tape it together.
6. Tape or glue the paper tube to the back of the lamp for a stand.
7. Stand the lamp up and read the Bible verse on it.

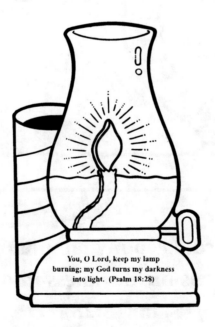

You, O Lord, keep my lamp
burning; my God turns my darkness
into light. (Psalm 18:28)

Finished Product

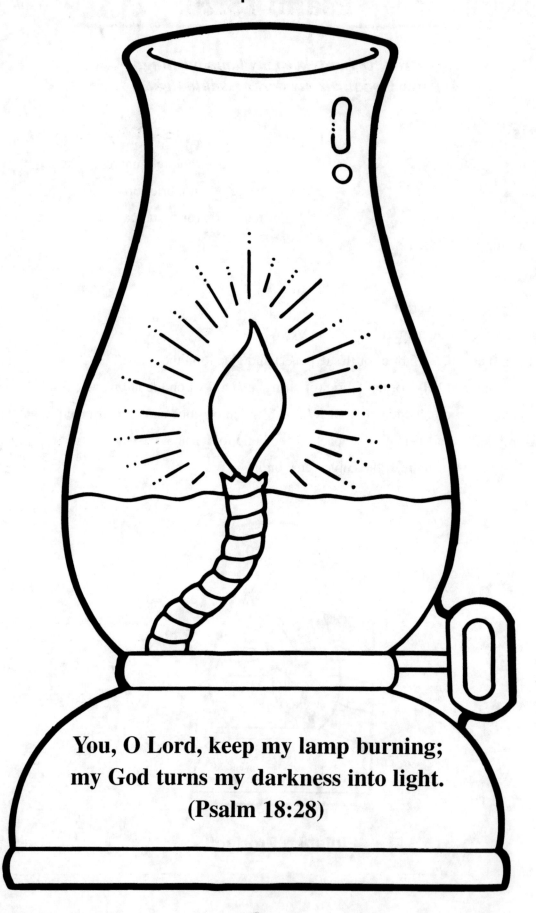

You, O Lord, keep my lamp burning;
my God turns my darkness into light.
(Psalm 18:28)

Psalm 19:14

"May the words of my mouth and the meditation of my heart be pleasing in your sight, O Lord, my Rock and my Redeemer."

Materials

- pattern (below)
- crayons or colored markers
- cardstock
- scissors
- clear adhesive plastic
- hole punch
- thin yarn

Directions

1. Copy the bookmark pattern on cardstock.
2. Color and cut out the pattern.
3. Cover the pattern, front and back, with clear adhesive plastic.
4. Punch a hole in the top of the bookmark.
5. Tie a piece of yarn in the hole. Fringe the ends of the yarn.
6. Keep the bookmark in your Bible to help you memorize the Bible verse.

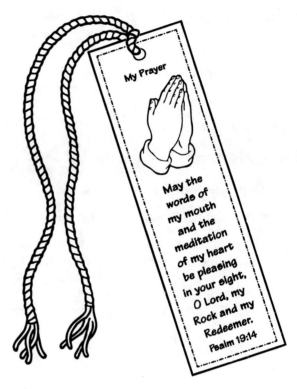

Finished Product

Bookmark Pattern

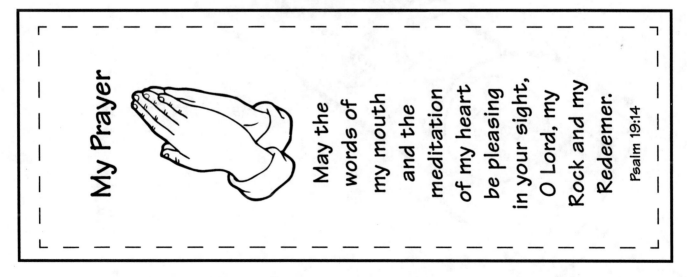

Psalm 27:1a

"The Lord is my light and my salvation—whom shall I fear?"

Materials

- pattern (below)
- crayons or colored markers
- cardstock
- scissors

Directions

1. Copy the bookmark on cardstock.
2. Color the bookmark and cut it out.
3. Put the bookmark in your favorite book or in your Bible at your favorite Bible story.

Finished Product

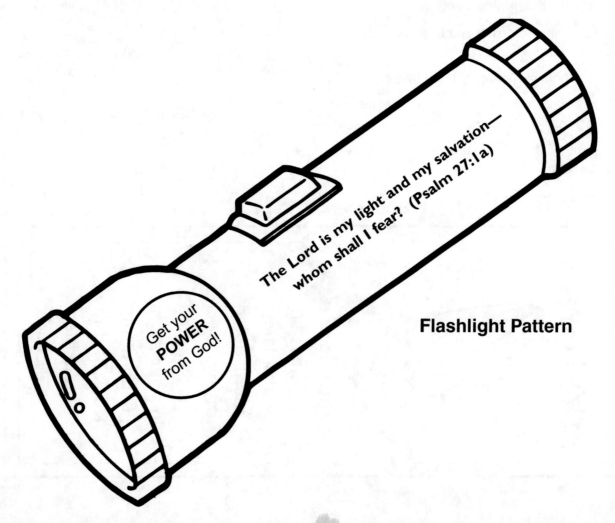

The Lord is my light and my salvation—whom shall I fear? (Psalm 27:1a)

Get your **POWER** from God!

Flashlight Pattern

Psalm 29:11

"The Lord gives strength to his people;
the Lord blesses his people with peace."

Materials

- pattern (page 36)
- crayons or colored markers
- cardstock
- scissors
- tape

Directions

1. Copy the pattern on cardstock.
2. Color and cut out the pattern. Draw your own designs on the pattern (hearts, crosses, flowers, etc.).
3. Fold the pattern on the dashed lines.
4. Tape the ends of the pattern together so it will stand up.
5. Read the first part of the Bible verse on the STRENGTH side of the stand-up, then turn it around and read the rest of the verse on the PEACE side. Turn it once more to read where the verse is found in the Bible.

Finished Product

The Lord gives

STRENGH

to his people;

the Lord blesses his people with

PEACE.

Psalm 29:11

36

Psalm 32:8

"I will instruct you and teach you in the way you should go;
I will counsel you and watch over you."

Materials

- pattern (page 38)
- colored cardstock
- scissors
- tape

Directions

1. Copy the pattern on colored cardstock.

2. Cut out the pattern. Be sure to cut out the slit in the section after 12 and before the clasp at the end.

3. Tape the two pieces together between the 7th and 8th sections.

4. Accordion fold the sections on the dashed lines.

5. Wrap the last longer section around the folded sections and slip the clasp into the slit to hold the Bible verse mini-book together.

6. Open the mini-book to read and memorize the Bible verse.

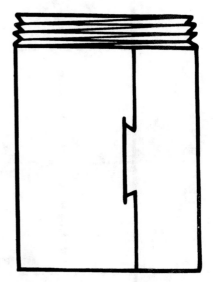

Closed Finished Product

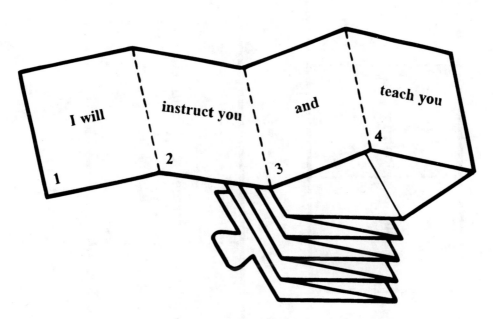

Opened Finished Product

Mini Book Pattern

go;

7

you should

6

in the way

5

teach you

4

and

3

instruct you

2

I will

1

(Psalm 32:8)

12

over you.

11

and watch

10

counsel you

9

I will

8

Psalm 37:4

"Delight yourself in the Lord
and he will give you the desires of your heart."

Materials

- pattern (below)
- cardstock
- glue
- 2.5" x 17.5" strip of colored paper
- memory verse word strips (below)
- ruler
- scissors
- pencil

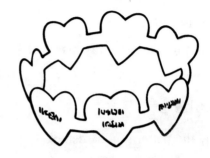

Finished Product

Directions

1. Copy the patterns on cardstock. Cut them out.

2. Using a ruler, make a small mark on the colored strip every 2.5 inches.

3. Accordion fold the strip of colored paper seven times where marked.

4. Trace around the heart pattern on the folded paper. The right and left edges of the pattern should rest on the folds of the paper.

5. Cut out the hearts. Do not cut on the fold lines. Unfold the hearts.

6. Cut out the memory verse word strips.

7. Glue the word strips on the hearts in correct order.

8. Glue the ends of the connected hearts together and stand them up to read the memory verse.

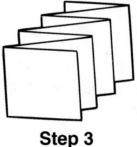

Step 3

Step 4

Verse Pattern

Delight yourself

in the Lord

and he will

give you

the desires

of your heart.

(Psalm 37:4)

Heart Pattern

Psalm 46:1

"God is our refuge and strength, an ever-present help in trouble."

Materials

- patterns (below)
- colored markers or crayons
- hole punch
- cardstock
- scissors
- string

Directions

1. Copy the pattern on cardstock.
2. Color and cut out the pattern.
3. Punch a hole in the top of the "GOD" pattern and also in the bottom of the "O." Punch a hole in the top of the Bible verse card.
4. Tie string in the hole at the top of the Bible verse card and attach it to the bottom hole of the "GOD" pattern as shown.
5. Tie string in the hole at the top of the "GOD" pattern and hang it in a window.

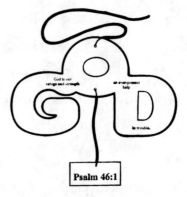

Finished Product

Psalm 46:1

"GOD" Pattern

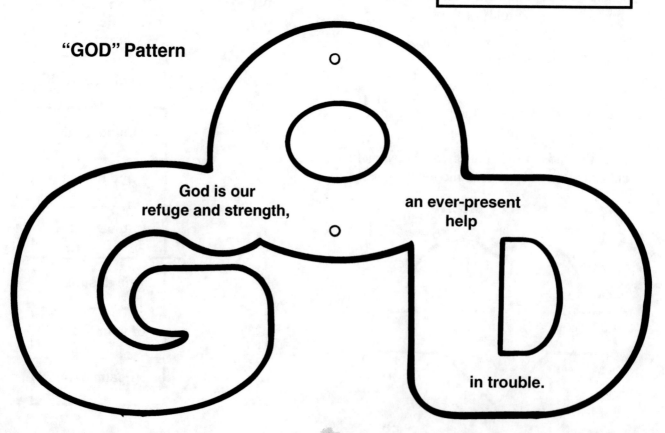

God is our refuge and strength,

an ever-present help

in trouble.

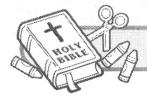

Psalm 46:10a

"'Be still and know that I am God.'"

Materials

- patterns (below and on page 42)
- cardstock
- colored markers or crayons
- scissors
- glue
- silver glitter
- clear adhesive plastic

Directions

1. Copy the patterns on cardstock.
2. Color the picture. Color the framing stick pieces brown or gray.
3. Cut out the picture and the framing sticks.
4. Spread a thin layer of glue on the snow on the mountain tops and sprinkle glitter over them. Shake off excess.
5. Carefully cover the picture with clear adhesive plastic.
6. Glue the sticks along the four sides of the picture for a frame.

Frame Patterns

Finished Product

"Be still and know that I am God."
(Psalm 46:10a)

42

Psalm 51:10

"Create in me a pure heart, O God,
and renew a steadfast spirit within me."

Materials

- pattern (below)
- colored markers or crayons
- colored envelope
- heart stickers
- pencil
- cardstock
- scissors

Directions

1. Copy the heart pattern onto cardstock and cut it out.
2. Trace the heart pattern on the corner edge of an envelope.
3. Cut out the heart, being careful not to cut through the folded edge of the envelope.
4. Outline the heart on both sides with crayon or marker.
5. Print the Bible verse on one side of the heart:

   "Create in me a pure heart, O God, and renew a steadfast spirit within me." (Psalm 51:10)
6. Decorate the heart on both sides with your own designs and heart stickers.
7. To use the heart as a bookmark, slip it over the bottom corner of a page in your book or Bible.

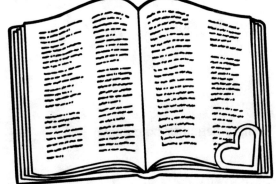

Finished Product

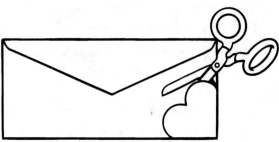

Steps 2 and 3

Step 4

Heart Pattern

Psalm 56:11

"In God I trust; I will not be afraid. What can man do to me?"

Materials

- pattern (below)
- colored markers or crayons
- cardstock
- scissors
- sharp pencil or hole punch
- clear tape
- rubber band (or string)

Directions

1. Copy the pattern on cardstock.
2. Color and cut out the pattern.
3. Place a small piece of clear tape at each end of the watch to keep it from tearing. Wrap around any excess.
4. Use a sharp pencil or a hole punch to punch a small hole near each end of the pattern where the tape covers.
5. Attach a rubber band to each hole. Loop the rubber band through one hole, then back through itself. Then loop the other end through the second hole and tie a knot in the end, big enough to keep it from slipping back through the hole. (You may prefer to tie string in the holes rather than a rubber band.)
6. Put the bracelet on your wrist and read the Bible verse. Wear it as a reminder that God is taking care of you all the time.

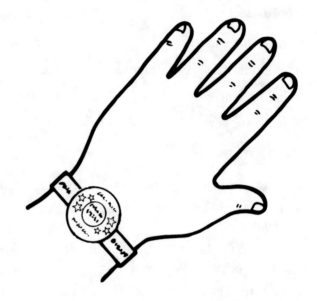

Finished Product

Watch Pattern

Psalm 84:11

"For the Lord God is a sun and shield; the Lord bestows favor and honor;
no good thing does he withhold from those whose walk is blameless."

Materials

- pattern (below)
- cardboard
- paint and paintbrush
- scissors
- pencil
- yarn
- aluminum foil
- dry cloth
- dark marker
- glue

Directions

1. Copy the shield pattern and cut it out.

2. Trace around the shield on cardboard and cut it out.

3. Using a pencil, draw a design on the shield (sword, cross, Bible, heart, etc.). Draw an outline of the shield around it.

4. Go over the pencil design with glue, then carefully press yarn on the design lines.

5. Let the glue dry; then cover the shield with aluminum foil. (Slightly crumple the foil, then unfold to make the shield look old.) Tuck the foil in and around the yarn design.

6. Paint the whole shield.

7. Using a dry cloth, gently wipe off much of the paint, leaving it in the wrinkles and crevices. Let dry.

8. Print Psalm 84:11 on the back of your shield with a marker.

Finished Product

Shield Pattern

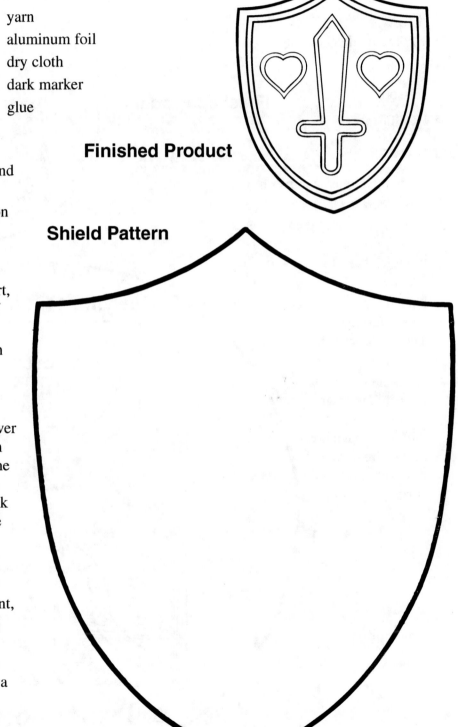

Psalm 86:15

"But you, O Lord, are a compassionate and gracious God, slow to anger, abounding in love and faithfulness."

Materials

- patterns (this page and page 47)
- colored markers or crayons
- cardstock
- scissors
- brad fastener

Directions

1. Copy the circle patterns on cardstock.

2. Color and cut out the two circles. Be sure to cut out the triangle-shaped window in the first one.

3. Attach the circles together with a brad fastener at the center. The circle with the window should be on the top.

4. Read the words of the Bible verse in numbered order through the window of the circle to discover some attributes of God.

Finished Product

Front of Wheel

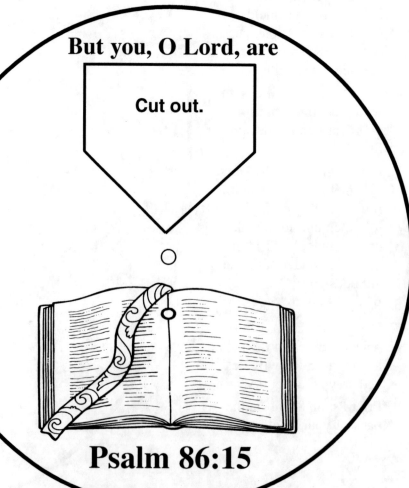

Cut out.

But you, O Lord, are

Psalm 86:15

Back of Wheel

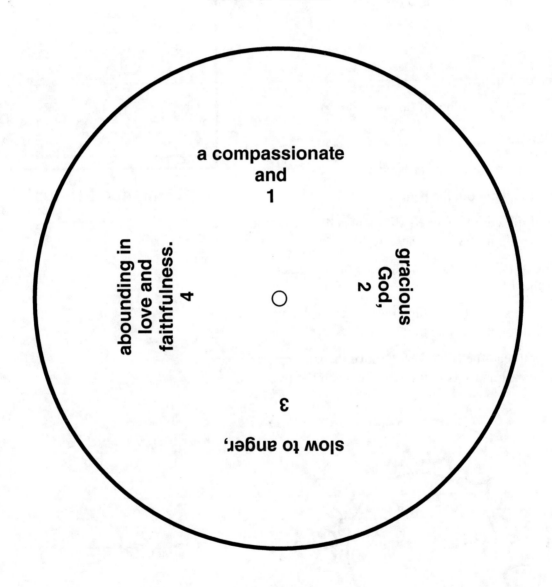

a compassionate
and
1

gracious
God,
2

abounding in
love and
faithfulness.
4

3
slow to anger,

Psalm 103:12

*"As far as the east is from the west,
so far has he removed our transgressions from us."*

Materials

- patterns (below and page 49)
- colored markers or crayons
- cardstock
- scissors
- tape or glue
- craft stick or cardboard (about 3" long)

Directions

1. Copy the patterns on cardstock.

2. Color and cut out the patterns.

3. Carefully cut two curved slits across the top of the picture along the dark lines.

4. Glue or tape the sun to a 3" piece of craft stick or cardboard.

5. Add the sun to the picture, carefully inserting the stick through the slits to the back.

6. As you read the Bible verse, move the sun so it rises in the east and sets in the west between the two slits.

Finished Product

Sun Pattern

As far as the east is from the west, so far has he removed our transgressions from us. (Psalm 103:12)

Psalm 103:13

*"As a father has compassion on his children,
so the Lord has compassion on those who fear him."*

Materials

- patterns (below)
- colored markers or crayons
- tape or glue
- scissors
- cardstock
- string or yarn
- hole punch

Directions

1. Copy the patterns on cardstock.
2. Color each circle and the Bible verse card and cut them out.
3. Tape or glue the circles together to spell COMPASSION.
4. Tape the top circle to the Bible verse card.
5. Punch holes at top corners. Tie string to the card for a hanger.

Finished Product

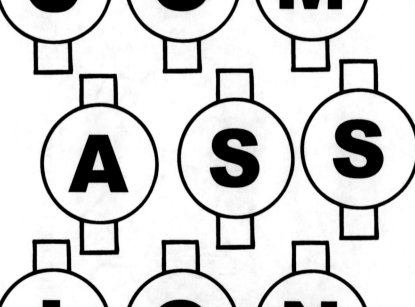

As a father has compassion on his children, so the Lord has compassion on those who fear him. (Psalm 103:13)

Psalm 118:24

"This is the day the Lord has made; let us rejoice and be glad in it."

Materials

- pattern (page 52)
- cardstock
- tape
- string
- colored markers or crayons
- scissors
- crépe paper streamers or strips of colored fabric
- hole punch

Directions

1. Copy the pattern on cardstock.
2. Color and cut out the pattern.
3. Tape crépe paper or fabric streamers to the bottom of the back of the pattern.
4. Roll the pattern into a tube and tape the ends together securely.
5. Punch small holes on two sides of the mini-windsock and attach string for a hanger.
6. Hang the mini-windsock outside on a porch or inside near an open window where a breeze can blow it around and remind you to rejoice in the Lord every day.

Finished Product

This is the day the Lord
has made; let us
REJOICE
and be glad in it.
(Psalm 118:24)

52

Psalm 119:89

"Your word, O Lord, is eternal; it stands firm in the heavens."

Materials

- patterns (below)
- glitter
- cardstock
- scissors
- glue
- dark blue or black construction paper

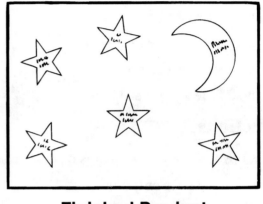

Finished Product

Directions

1. Copy the patterns on cardstock.
2. Lightly smear glue on each star and sprinkle glitter on them. Shake off the excess glitter.
3. Cut out the stars and the moon.
4. Glue the stars and moon on dark blue or black construction paper in correct order.
5. Read the words on the stars and the moon to learn the memory verse.

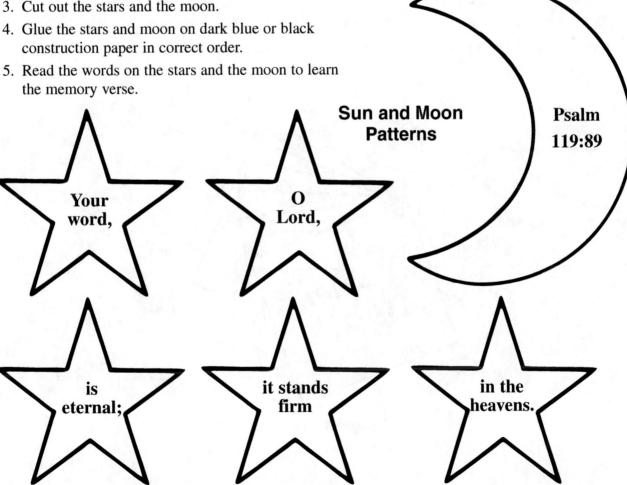

Sun and Moon Patterns

Your word,

O Lord,

Psalm 119:89

is eternal;

it stands firm

in the heavens.

Psalm 119:105

"Your word is a lamp to my feet and a light for my path."

Materials

- patterns (page 55)
- crayons or colored markers
- clear adhesive plastic
- brad fastener or metal ring
- scissors
- cardstock
- hole punch

Directions

1. Copy the word card patterns on cardstock.

2. Color the six word cards.

3. Cover the word cards with clear adhesive plastic, front and back.

4. Cut the word cards apart and stack them in numbered order.

5. Punch a hole in the top left corner of the stack.

6. Fasten the six cards together in the numbered order with a brad fastener or metal ring.

7. Memorize Psalm 119:105 by going through the words on the cards.

Finished Product

Psalm 119:105

1

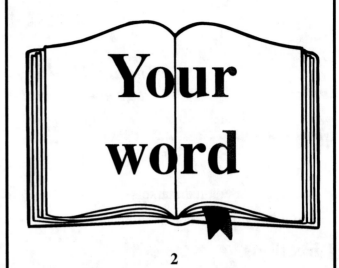
Your word

2

is a lamp

3

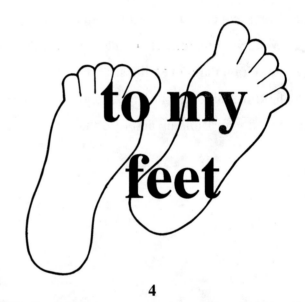
to my feet

4

and a light

5

for my path

6

Psalm 119:130

"The unfolding of your words gives light;
it gives understanding to the simple."

Materials

- pattern (page 57)
- crayons or colored markers
- gold or silver pen or fine-tipped marker
- scissors
- cardstock
- glue

Directions

1. Copy the Bible pattern on cardstock.
2. Color and cut out the Bible pattern.
3. Write your name on the bottom part of the cover of the Bible in gold or silver.
4. Fold it on the broken lines.
5. Fold the tab back and glue it under the cover of the Bible.
6. Stand your Bible up and read the memory verse.

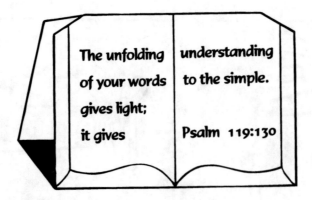

The unfolding of your words gives light; it gives

understanding to the simple.

Psalm 119:130

Finished Product

name

Holy Bible

The unfolding | understanding

of your words | to the simple.

gives light;

it gives | Psalm 119:130

Psalm 121:3–4

"He will not let your foot slip—he who watches over you will not slumber; indeed, he who watches over Israel will neither slumber nor sleep."

Materials

- patterns (page 59)
- cardstock
- cotton fabric (or large construction paper) at least 8" x 17"
- colored felt scraps
- crayons or colored markers
- carbon paper
- glue
- scissors
- wooden dowel
- string
- pen or pencil

Finished Product

Directions

1. Copy the patterns on cardstock and cut them out.

2. Trace around the patterns on colored felt scraps and cut them out.

3. Cut a few inches at the bottom of the fabric (or paper) banner into a V-shape or a fringed edge.

4. Using a pencil, trace the box on the fabric (or paper) where you will put the Bible verses. Sketch a design around the verse and on the rest of the fabric, using the design patterns from page 59.

5. Place a sheet of carbon paper over the fabric and put the Bible verse card over it. Use a pen or pencil to go over the letters firmly so they are transferred to the fabric. Then color them with markers. (If you're using paper for your banner, you can just color the Bible verse card and glue it on the banner.)

6. Glue felt patterns on the banner in the design you have sketched.

7. Fold the top of the banner over a wooden dowel and glue it down.

8. Tie a string to each end of the dowel to hang your banner.

He will not let your foot slip—he who watches over you will not slumber; indeed, he who watches over Israel will neither slumber nor sleep. (Psalm 121:3–4)

Psalm 139:14a

"I praise you because I am fearfully and wonderfully made."

Materials

- pattern (below)
- crayons or colored markers
- magnetic tape
- photo of yourself
- scissors
- cardstock
- glue
- gummed stars

Finished Product

Directions

1. Copy the frame pattern on cardstock.

2. Color and cut out the frame pattern.
   Be sure to cut out the center of the frame.

3. Add gummed stars to the design on the frame.

4. Cut out a cardstock square slightly larger than the cut-out portion of the frame and glue it to the back of the frame at the sides and bottom. Leave the top open.

5. Glue a piece of magnetic tape on the back of the frame.

6. Slip a photograph of yourself into the frame and attach it to your family's refrigerator door.

Frame Pattern

Psalm 139:23–24

"Search me, O God, and know my heart; test me and know my anxious thoughts. See if there is any offensive way in me, and lead me in the way everlasting."

Materials

- pattern (below)
- crayons or colored markers
- tape
- scissors
- cardstock

Finished Product

Directions

1. Copy the pattern on cardstock.
2. Color the pattern and cut it out.
3. Fold the pattern on the broken lines and tape the sides together to make a cube.
4. Read the Bible verses in numbered order on the sides of the cube.
5. Toss the cube down. Try to say the verses using the clue words that appear. Keep throwing the cube and saying the verses until you can say them without any help.

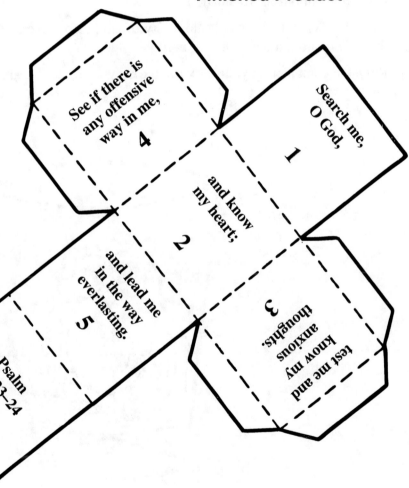

Cube Pattern

Proverbs 3:5–6

"Trust in the Lord with all your heart and lean not on your own understanding; in all your ways acknowledge him, and he will make your paths straight."

Materials

- pattern (page 63)
- crayons or colored markers
- plastic or Styrofoam™ container (3" to 4" in diameter)
- rubber band *(optional)*
- scissors
- cardstock
- glue

Directions

1. Copy the owl pattern on cardstock.

2. Color and cut out the owl pattern.

3. Glue the owl pattern on a plastic or Styrofoam™ container. (*Optional:* Use a rubber band to hold the pattern around the container until the glue sets.)

4. Keep the container on your desk to hold crayons or candy, and to remind you to trust the Lord.

Finished Product

Owl Pattern

in all your ways
acknowledge him,
and he will make
your paths straight.
(Proverbs 3:5–6)

Be
Wise

Trust in the Lord
with all your heart
and lean not on
your own
understanding;

Proverbs 13:3

*"He who guards his lips guards his life,
but he who speaks rashly will come to ruin."*

Materials

- patterns (below)
- red construction paper
- tape and glue
- scissors
- cardstock
- paper plate

Directions

1. Copy the lip patterns on red construction paper and cut them out.

2. Fold the paper plate in half with the bottom up.

3. Copy the Bible verse strip on cardstock and cut it out.

4. Glue the Bible verse strip on the inside of the folded plate near the fold line.

5. Fold back the top and bottom rim (about 1") of the folded plate near the outer center/middle.

6. Glue the red paper lips to the folded back rims, top and bottom, to make a mouth.

7. Cut out two strips of cardstock and tape the edges to the back of the folded plate for a place to put your thumb (bottom) and fingers (top) as you hold the plate. (See picture above.)

8. Make the mouth say the Bible verse along with you by pressing the plate halves together up and down.

Finished Product

Verse Pattern

He who guards his lips guards his life,
but he who speaks rashly will come to ruin.

(Proverbs 13:3)

Lips Pattern

Proverbs 15:1

"A gentle answer turns away wrath, but a harsh word stirs up anger."

Materials

- patterns (below)
- crayons or colored markers
- cardboard tube (toilet paper tube or a 1/3 of a paper towel tube)
- glue
- scissors
- cardstock

Directions

1. Copy the patterns on cardstock.
2. Color and cut out the patterns.
3. Cut a section about 3" long from a cardboard tube.
4. Glue the two patterns back to back with the cardboard tube in the middle.
5. Read the first part of the Bible verse on the first side of the figure; then turn it to the other side to read the rest of the verse.

Finished Product

but a harsh word stirs up anger.
(Proverbs 15:1)

Pattern (Back)

Pattern (Front)

A gentle answer turns away wrath,

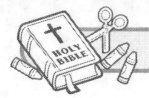

Proverbs 15:3

*"The eyes of the Lord are everywhere,
keeping watch on the wicked and the good."*

Materials

- pattern (below)
- crayons or colored markers
- colored cardstock
- cardboard (about 5" square)
- rags or paper towels
- black watercolor paint and paintbrush
- scissors
- aluminum foil
- glue
- magnetic strip

Directions

1. Copy the Bible verse pattern on colored cardstock and cut it out.

2. Cut out the center of a 5" square of cardboard to make a frame. The cut-out opening should be at least 3" square.

3. Crumple a sheet of aluminum foil, then smooth it out somewhat. (Leave some of the wrinkles and grooves.) Cover the frame, front and back, with the foil. Glue the foil on the back of the frame to secure it.

4. Paint over the foil with black water color paint. Then wipe off much of the paint with a rag or paper towel, leaving it in the wrinkles and grooves of the foil.

5. Glue the Bible verse pattern to the back of the frame so the verse shows through.

6. Glue a magnetic strip on the back so you can keep this reminder on the family refrigerator. It will remind you that God is with you.

Finished Product

Verse Pattern

The eyes of the
Lord are
everywhere,
keeping watch
on the wicked
and the good.
(Proverbs 15:3)

Ecclesiastes 12:1a

"Remember your Creator in the days of your youth."

Materials

- patterns (below)
- cardstock
- crayons or colored markers
- scissors
- tape

Finished Product

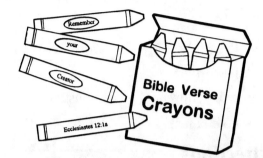

Crayon Box Pattern

Directions

1. Copy the patterns on cardstock.
2. Color and cut out the patterns. Color each crayon a different color. Cut each crayon apart.
3. Fold the crayon box pattern on the dashed lines and tape the sides together.
4. Put the eight crayons in the box.
5. Take out the crayons and place them in correct order to read the Bible verse.

Crayon Patterns

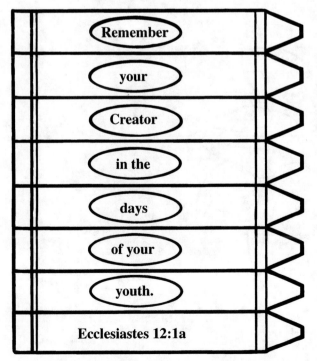

Remember

your

Creator

in the

days

of your

youth.

Ecclesiastes 12:1a

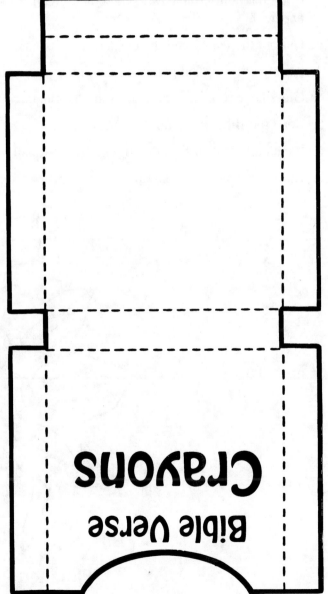

Bible Verse Crayons

Isaiah 9:6

"For to us a child is born, to us a son is given, and the government will be on his shoulders. And he will be called Wonderful Counselor, Mighty God, Everlasting Father, Prince of Peace."

Materials

- pattern (page 69)
- paper plate
- red, yellow, and green construction paper
- hole punch

- scissors
- string
- glue

Directions

1. Copy the poinsettia leaves on red and green construction paper and the small blossoms on yellow paper.

2. Cut out the leaves and the cluster of blossoms.

3. Arrange the red and green leaves on the paper plate to spell out the memory verse.

4. Glue the leaves onto the plate and glue the cluster of blossoms at the center of the plant.

5. Read the Bible verse on the poinsettia.

6. Punch a hole near the edge of one leaf. Attach a piece of string.

7. Hang your memory verse plant in a window after you memorize the verses.

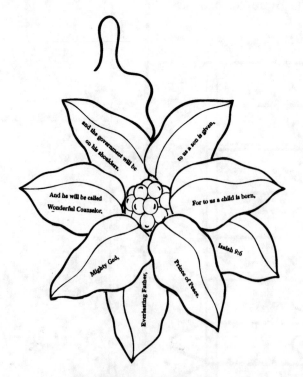

Finished Product

Poinsettia Patterns

Prince of Peace.

Isaiah 9:6

Everlasting Father,

Mighty God,

And he will be called Wonderful Counselor,

For to us a child is born,

to us a son is given,

and the government will be on his shoulders.

#7062 Bible Memory Verse Crafts

Isaiah 40:31

"But those who hope in the Lord will renew their strength.
They will soar on wings like eagles; they will run and not grow weary,
they will walk and not be faint."

Materials

- pattern (page 71)
- string
- colored markers or crayons
- scissors
- white paper
- tape
- hole punch
- small paper clip *(optional)*

Directions

1. Copy the eagle pattern on white paper.

2. Color and cut out the eagle. (Look in an encyclopedia or bird identification book to find out what colors it should be.)

3. Fold the eagle down the center and tape the two halves together under the head and at the bottom of the tail. Do not tape the wings together.

4. Fold up the wings and tail so the eagle looks like it is flying.

5. Use a hole punch to poke a small hole in the top of the eagle's back, near the middle of the wings.

6. Tie a piece of string in the hole.

7. Hold on to the string and fly your eagle around as you read the Bible verse on its wings.

    (*Hint:* To make the eagle fly straighter, place a small paper clip under its head.)

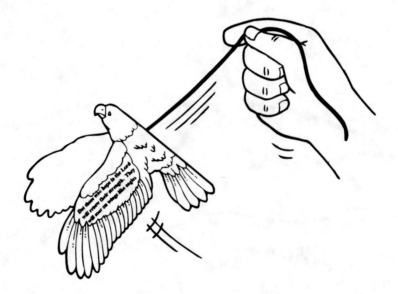

Finished Product

Eagle Pattern

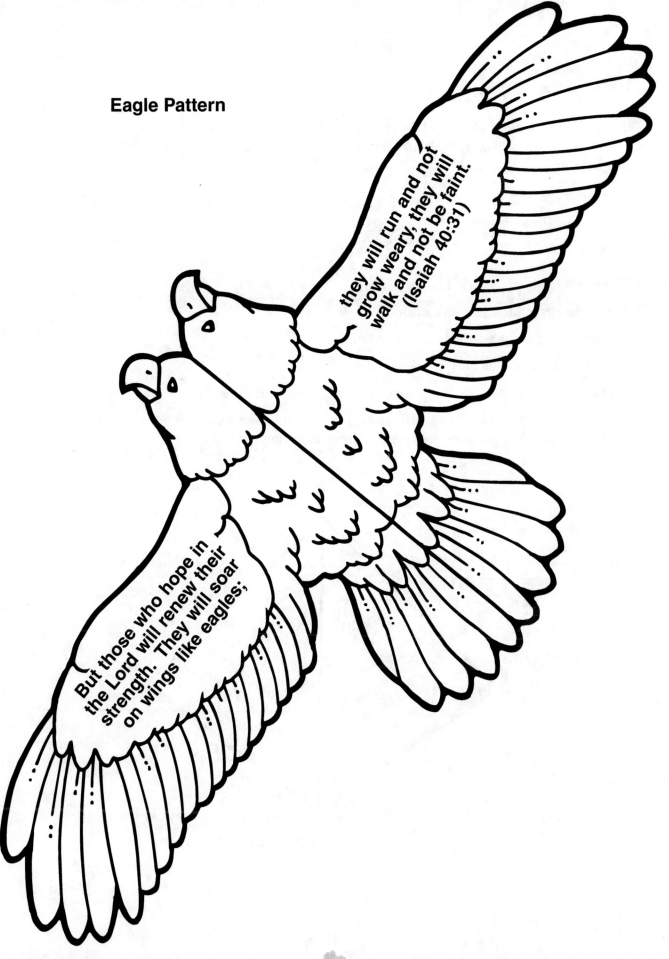

they will run and not grow weary, they will walk and not be faint. (Isaiah 40:31)

But those who hope in the Lord will renew their strength. They will soar on wings like eagles;

Isaiah 41:10

"'So do not fear, for I am with you; do not be dismayed,
for I am your God. I will strengthen you and help you;
I will uphold you with my righteous right hand.'"

Materials

- pattern (page 73)
- colored markers or crayons
- glue or tape
- cardstock
- scissors

Directions

1. Copy the pyramid pattern on cardstock.

2. Color and cut out the pattern.

3. Fold the pattern on the dashed lines.

4. Fold back the tab and glue it to the inside edge of the fourth triangle to make a stand-up pyramid.

5. Read the memory verse as you turn the pyramid around. Memorize the verse so you will have it in your mind when you need some encouragement during hard times.

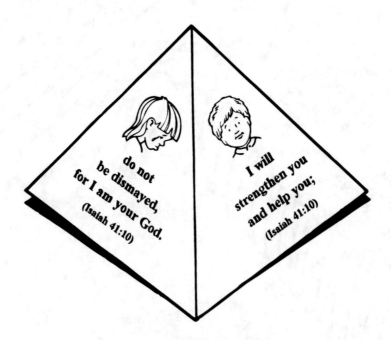

Finished Product

Pyramid Pattern

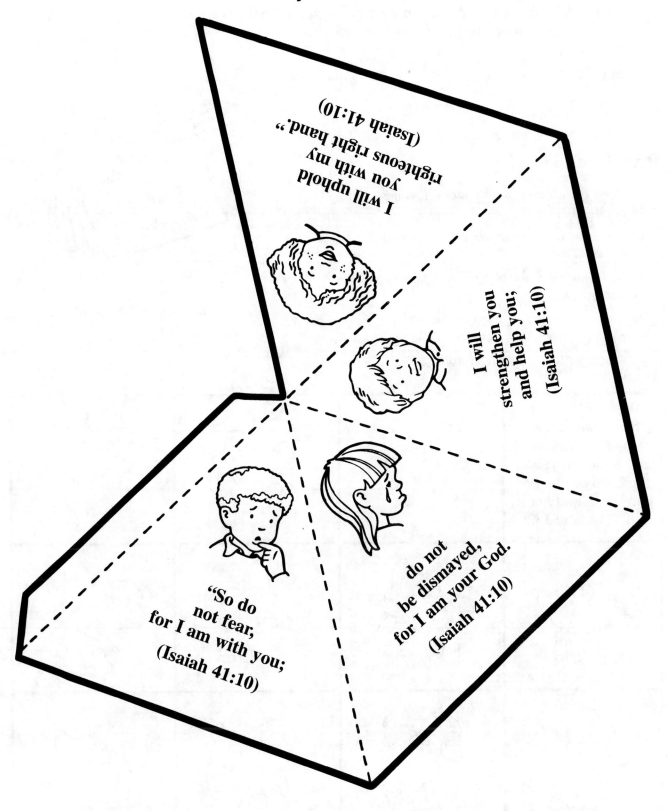

"I will uphold you with my righteous right hand." (Isaiah 41:10)

I will strengthen you and help you; (Isaiah 41:10)

"So do not fear, for I am with you; (Isaiah 41:10)

do not be dismayed, for I am your God. (Isaiah 41:10)

Isaiah 53:6

"We all, like sheep, have gone astray, each of us has turned to his own way; and the Lord has laid on him the iniquity of us all."

Materials

- patterns (below)
- stapler and staples
- scissors
- white copy paper

Directions

1. Copy the sheep pattern pages on white paper and cut them apart.
2. Stack the pages in numbered order with the Bible verse on top.
3. Make sure that the bottom of the pattern pages line up evenly.
4. Staple the pages together at the top.
5. Read the Bible verse; then flip quickly through the pages to see the sheep run.

Finished Product

We all, like sheep, have gone astray, each of us has turned to his own way; and the Lord has laid on him the iniquity of us all. (Isaiah 53:6)	1	2	3
4	5	6	7
8	9	10	11

Isaiah 55:8–9

"'For my thoughts are not your thoughts, neither are your ways my ways,' declares the Lord. 'As the heavens are higher than the earth, so are my ways higher than your ways, and my thoughts than your thoughts.'"

Materials

- pattern (below)
- scissors
- colored paper
- pencil

Directions

1. Copy the flower pattern on colored paper.

2. Cut out the flower pattern.

3. Fold each petal toward the center of the flower. Do not let the petals cover the flower center.

4. Use a pencil to write numbers on the back of the petals to remind you which ones to open first to keep the words of the Bible verse in order.

5. Unfold the petals one at a time and read the Bible verse words in correct order. Read the Bible book reference in the center of the flower last.

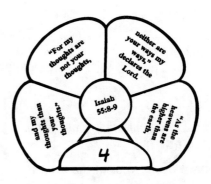

Finished Product

Flower Pattern

neither are your ways my ways," declares the Lord.

"For my thoughts are not your thoughts,

"As the heavens are higher than the earth,

Isaiah 55:8–9

and my thoughts than your thoughts."

so are my ways higher than your ways,

Jeremiah 29:11

"'For I know the plans I have for you,' declares the Lord, 'plans to prosper you and not to harm you, plans to give you hope and a future.'"

Materials

- patterns (below)
- construction paper
- glue
- stapler and staples
- scissors
- white paper
- colored markers or crayons

Directions

1. Make a copy of the calendar pattern for each month left in the year.
2. Write a month of the year at the top of each calendar. Then number the days. (Look at a current calendar to see on which day each month begins.)
3. Cut a piece of construction paper the same size as the calendars for a cover.
4. Put the calendars in order with the cover first and staple them together at the top.
5. Cut out the Bible verse and glue it on the calendar cover.
6. Keep your personal calendar in your Bible or in your desk at school. Try to memorize Jeremiah 29:11 before you use up all the calendars.

Calendar Pattern

Staple calendars together here.

Sun	Mon	Tues	Wed	Thurs	Fri	Sat

Verse Pattern

"For I know the plans I have for you," declares the Lord, "plans to prosper you and not to harm you, plans to give you hope and a future." (Jeremiah 29:11)

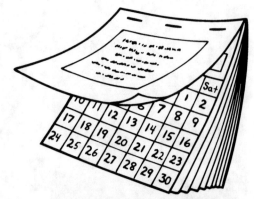

Finished Product

76

Jeremiah 31:3

"The Lord appeared to us in the past, saying: 'I have loved you with an everlasting love; I have drawn you with loving-kindness.'"

Materials

- pattern (page 78)
- colored markers or crayons
- business envelope
- scissors
- cardstock

Directions

1. Copy the puzzle pattern on cardstock.

2. Color and cut out the puzzle. Cut it into 12 pieces.

3. Write the Bible verse reference, Jeremiah 31:3, on the back of an envelope.

4. Keep the puzzle pieces in the envelope.

5. Practice saying the verse every time you put the puzzle together until you have it memorized.

Finished Product

The Lord appeared to us in the past, saying: "I have loved you with an everlasting love; I have drawn you with loving-kindness." (Jeremiah 31:3)

Jeremiah 33:3

"'Call to me and I will answer you and tell you great and unsearchable things you do not know.'"

Materials

- pattern (below)
- colored cardstock
- scissors

Directions

1. Copy the cell phone pattern on colored cardstock.
2. Cut out the phone pattern.
3. Fold the phone on the broken line.
4. Open the phone and read the Bible verse.
5. Aren't you glad you don't really have to use a phone to hear from God? How does He talk to you?

Finished Product

Phone Pattern

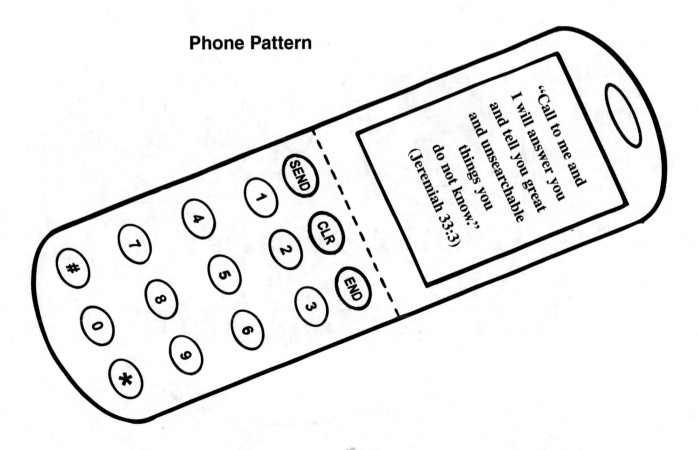

"Call to me and I will answer you and tell you great and unsearchable things you do not know." (Jeremiah 33:3)

Zephaniah 3:17

"'The Lord your God is with you, he is mighty to save.
He will take great delight in you, he will quiet you with his love,
he will rejoice over you with singing.'"

Materials

- patterns (this page and page 81)
- cardstock
- colored markers or crayons
- scissors
- hole punch
- brad fastener

Directions

1. Copy the circle patterns on cardstock.
2. Color the circles and cut them out.
3. Cut out the window in the cover circle.
4. Punch a hole in the center of each circle.
5. Put the two circles together, with the window circle on top, with a brad fastener.
6. Turn the bottom circle to read God's promises in Zephaniah 3:17. (Read them in numbered order.)

Finished Product

Circle Pattern (Front)

Circle
Pattern
(Back)

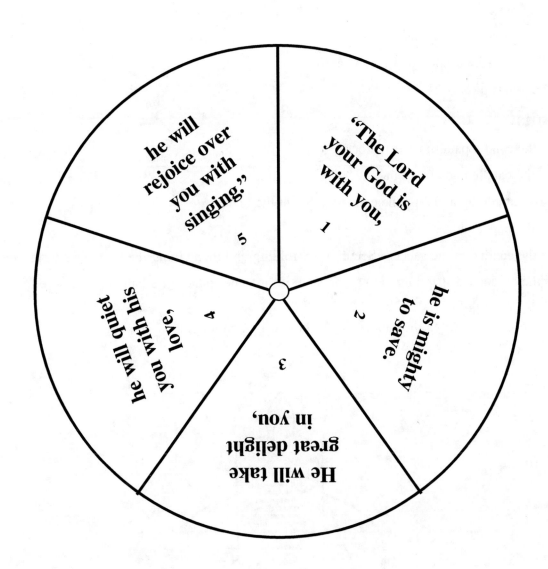

Matthew 5:16

"'In the same way, let your light shine before men,
that they may see your good deeds and praise your father in heaven.'"

Materials

- pattern (page 83)
- colored markers or crayons
- paper saucer (or cardboard circle, 5" across)
- cardboard strip (5" x 3/4")

- scissors
- cardstock
- tape

Directions

1. Copy the candle pattern on cardstock.

2. Color the candle and cut it out.

3. Roll the candle up and tape the ends together at the back.

4. Color the paper saucer.

5. Place the candle on the saucer. Secure it by folding and then taping the three tabs to the saucer.

6. Tape the cardboard strip in a loop at the side of the paper plate for a handle. (Be sure to tape it securely to the top and bottom of the plate.)

7. Read the Bible verse on the candle as you hold it up and let your light shine.

Finished Product

Candle Pattern

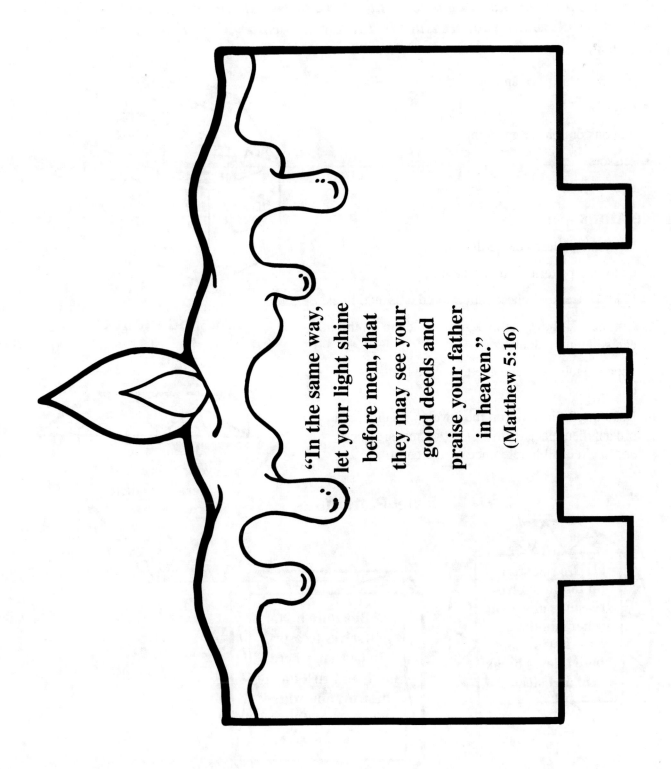

"In the same way, let your light shine before men, that they may see your good deeds and praise your father in heaven." (Matthew 5:16)

Matthew 6:19–21

"'Do not store up for yourselves treasures on earth, where moth and rust destroy, and where thieves break in and steal. But store up for yourselves treasures in heaven, where moth and rust do not destroy, and where thieves do not break in and steal. For where your treasure is, there your heart will be also.'"

Materials

- patterns (this page and page 85)
- cardstock
- crayons or colored markers
- scissors
- tape

Directions

1. Copy the patterns on cardstock.
2. Color the patterns and cut them out.
3. Fold the treasure chest pattern on the dashed lines.
4. Cut the slit above the lock so that the tab on the lid can slide in the lock.
5. Tape the tabs to the inside to secure the treasure chest.
6. Read the Bible verse on the jewels (in numbered order), then place them inside the treasure chest and say the Bible reference on the chest.

Finished Product

Jewel Patterns

3. For where your treasure is, there your heart will be also.

1. Do not store up for yourselves treasures on earth, where moth and rust destroy, and where thieves break in and steal.

2. But store up for yourselves treasures in heaven, where moth and rust do not destroy, and where thieves do not break in and steal.

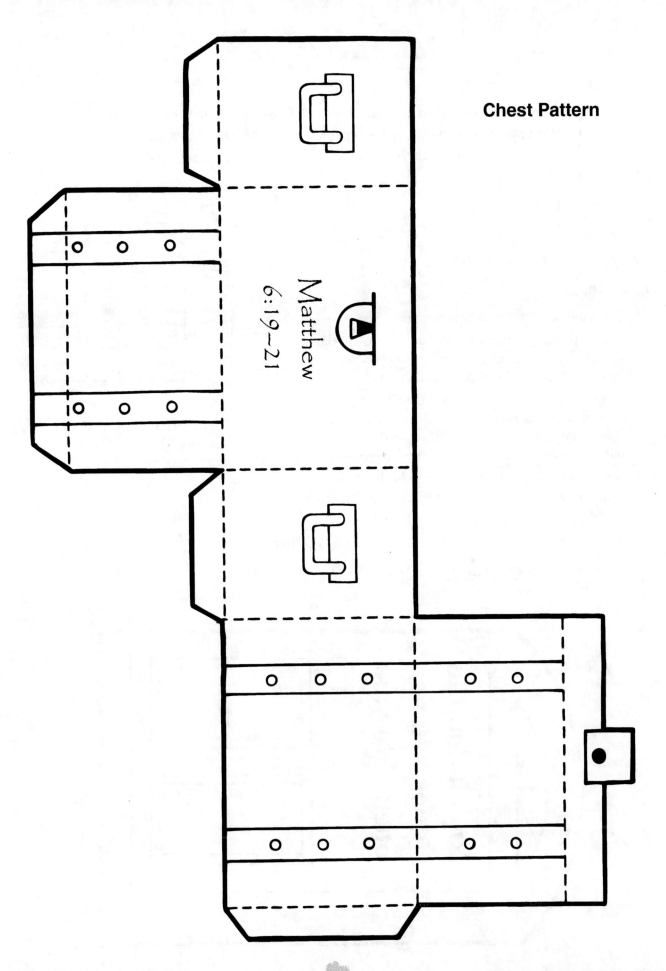

Chest Pattern

Matthew
6:19–21

"'Ask and it will be given to you; seek and you will find; knock and the door will be opened to you. For everyone who asks receives; he who seeks finds; and to him who knocks, the door will be opened.'"

Materials

- patterns (this page and page 87)
- scissors
- cardstock
- glue
- crayons or colored markers

Directions

1. Copy the patterns on cardstock.
2. Color and cut out the patterns. Be sure to cut the top and bottom of the door pattern as shown in the picture. Fold the door on the dashed line.
3. Glue the door to the house on page 87 over the door shape—only on the three sides that do not open. (Put glue only around the door frame, not on the door itself.) Allow time for the glue to dry.
4. Read the Bible verses on each side of the door, then on the door. Open the door and read the rest of the verses inside.

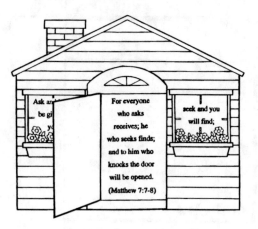

Finished Product

Door Pattern

Cut here.

Cut here.

knock and the door will be opened to you.

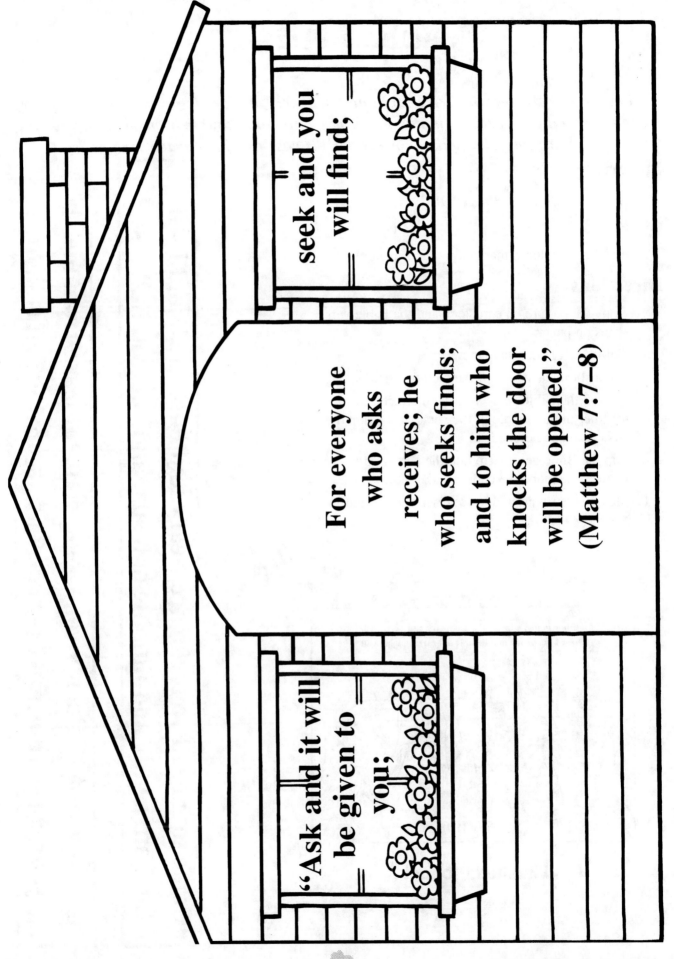

seek and you will find;

"For everyone who asks receives; he who seeks finds; and to him who knocks the door will be opened." (Matthew 7:7–8)

"Ask and it will be given to you;

Matthew 11:28–30

"'Come to me, all you who are weary and burdened, and I will give you rest. Take my yoke upon you and learn from me, for I am gentle and humble in heart, and you will find rest for your souls. For my yoke is easy and my burden is light.'"

Materials

- pattern (this page and page 89)
- cardstock
- crayons or colored markers
- scissors
- tape
- paper

Directions

1. Copy the picture on cardstock and the Bible verse strips on paper.
2. Color and cut out the picture.
3. Cut a slit in each side of the picture where shown.
4. Cut out the Bible verse strips and tape them together in the middle of the verse. (Overlap the ends and tape both sides.)
5. Slip the Bible verse strip into the slits on the picture, then tape the ends together at the back.
6. Move the strip around to read what Jesus said in Matthew 11:28–30.

Verse Strips

Finished Product

"Come to me, all you who are weary and burdened, and I will for I am gentle and humble in heart, and you will find rest

give you rest. Take my yoke upon you and learn from me, for your souls. For my yoke is easy and my burden is light."

Matthew 11:28–30

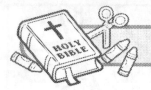

Luke 1:37

"'For nothing is impossible with God.'"

Materials

- pattern (below)
- cardstock
- crayons or colored markers
- wide blue ribbon
- scissors
- glue
- glitter

Directions

1. Copy the award pattern on cardstock.
2. Color and cut out the pattern.
3. Spread a thin layer of glue around the outer edge of the circle. Sprinkle glitter on the glue. Shake off the excess glitter.
4. Cut two pieces of ribbon, each about 6 ½" long.
5. Cut a "V" into the ribbons at the bottom. Glue the top end of each ribbon together and then glue them to the award circle at the bottom.
6. Memorize the Bible verse and let the blue ribbon remind you that you can do anything with God's help!

Finished Product

Award Pattern

"For nothing is impossible with God." (Luke 1:37)

Luke 6:37

"'Do not judge, and you will not be judged. Do not condemn,
and you will not be condemned. Forgive, and you will be forgiven.'"

Materials

- pattern (below)
- white paper
- crayons or colored markers
- scissors
- tape or glue

Finished Product

Directions

1. Copy the patterns on white paper.
2. Color and cut out the patterns. Be sure to cut around the windows on three sides. Fold on the dashed lines so the windows will flap open.
3. Glue or tape the key word pattern behind the Bible verse pattern.
4. As you read the Bible verse, open the windows to discover the key words.

Front Pattern   **Back Pattern**

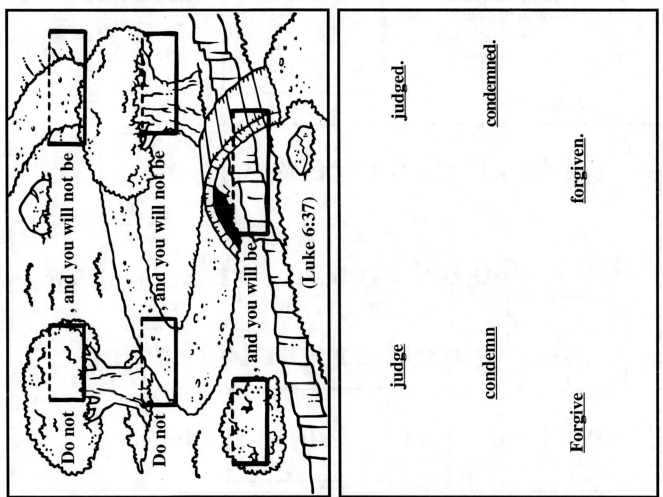

"Yet to all who received him, to those who believed in his name, he gave the right to become children of God."

Materials

- pattern (below)
- scissors
- cardstock
- tape
- crayons or colored markers

Finished Product

Directions

1. Copy the Bible verse and picture patterns on cardstock.
2. Color the patterns and cut them out.
3. Tape the pictures over the words of the verse. (See boxes.) Tape them only at the top so they can be lifted up to see the words underneath.
4. Memorize the Bible verse.

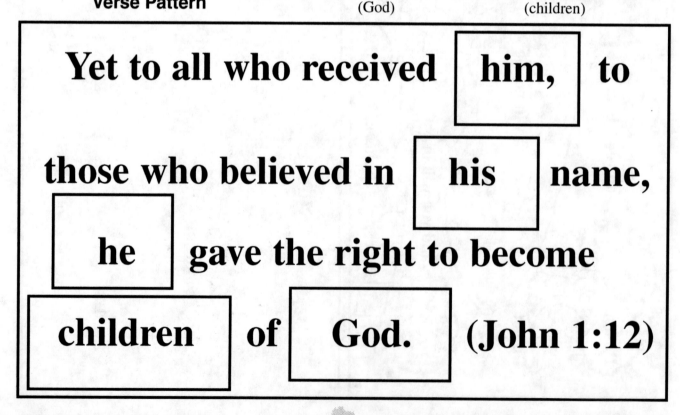

(him)   (his)   (he)

(God)   (children)

Verse Pattern

Yet to all who received | him, | to

those who believed in | his | name,

| he | gave the right to become

children | of | God. | (John 1:12)

John 3:16

"'For God so loved the world that he gave his one and only Son, that whoever believes in him shall not perish but have eternal life.'"

Materials

- patterns (this page and page 94)
- hole punch
- crayons or colored markers
- scissors
- thread or yarn
- cardstock

Directions

1. Copy the patterns on cardstock.
2. Color and cut out the patterns.
3. Punch five holes in the bottom of the earth pattern and one hole in each of the others.
4. On the backs of the five smaller patterns, print "I KNOW GOD LOVES ME," one word on each pattern. Print the words in numbered order as the words of the Bible verse appear.
5. Use various lengths of thread or yarn to tie the patterns to the large Earth pattern.
6. Punch a hole in the top of the earth pattern and tie a thread in it to hang.

Finished Product

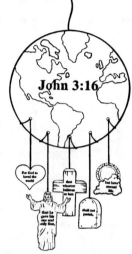

Jesus Pattern

that he gave his one and only Son,

Heart Pattern

"For God so loved the world

that whoever believes in him

but have eternal life."

shall not perish

John 3:16

Earth Pattern

John 10:11

"'I am the good shepherd. The good shepherd lays down his life for the sheep.'"

Materials

- patterns (below)
- cardstock and white paper
- crayons or colored markers
- scissors
- tape

Finished Product

Directions

1. Copy the pattern on cardstock and the Bible verse strip on regular white paper.

2. Color the patterns and cut the Bible verse strip. To cut out the shepherd and sheep pattern, fold the cardstock in half with the left side of the pattern on the fold. Cut around the pattern, not cutting through the fold. Be sure to cut out the spaces around the sheep.

3. Unfold the pattern and you will have the shepherd with his sheep.

4. Tape the Bible verse strip at the bottom of the shepherd and sheep piece.

5. Tape the ends of the pattern together to make a circular stand-up Bible verse reminder.

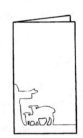

Step 2

"I am the good shepherd. The good shepherd lays down his life for the sheep."
(John 10:11)

Shepherd and Sheep Pattern

Step 3

John 14:6

"Jesus answered, 'I am the way and the truth and the life. No one comes to the Father except through me.'"

Materials

- patterns (below)
- cardstock
- crayons or colored markers
- clear adhesive plastic
- scissors
- hole punch
- brad fastener

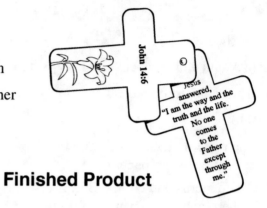

Finished Product

Directions

1. Copy the patterns on cardstock.

2. Color the patterns and cut them out.

3. Cover both crosses, front and back, with clear adhesive plastic. Trim extra plastic around the edges.

4. Punch a hole at the top of each cross. (Hold one cross on top of the other, as you do this, so the holes line up perfectly.)

5. Put a brad fastener in the holes to connect the two crosses. The cross with the Bible verse should go on the bottom.

6. Use the crosses to memorize the Bible verse.

Cross Patterns

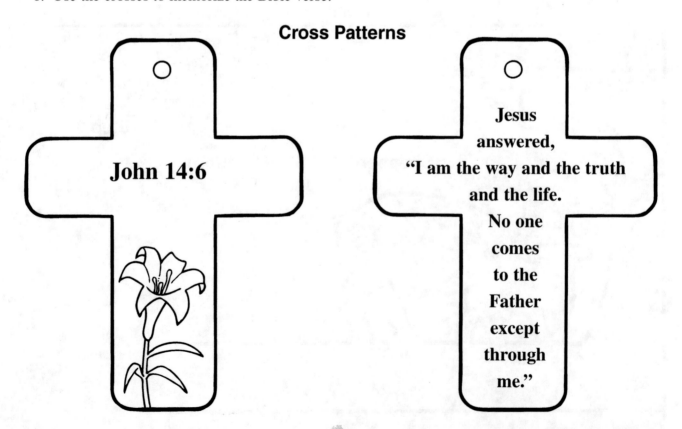

John 15:5b

"Apart from me you can do nothing."

Materials

- pattern (below)
- colored cardstock
- tissue paper of various colors
- clear adhesive plastic
- scissors
- string
- glue

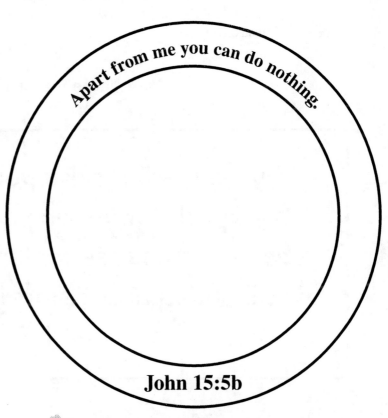

Finished Product

Directions

1. Make two copies of the pattern on colored cardstock.
2. Cut two circles of clear adhesive plastic and one of cardstock, all the same size as the pattern.
3. Cut out pieces of tissue paper of different colors, shapes, and sizes.
4. Lay the tissue paper pieces in a circle arrangement on the cardstock circle until it looks the way you want it to.
5. Move the tissue paper pieces onto the adhesive plastic circle in the same arrangement. Cover the whole circle.
6. Cover the design with the second adhesive plastic circle.
7. Cut out the inner circle of each cardstock pattern to make a "window."
8. Glue the two patterns to the front and back of the tissue paper circle, sandwiching it between them with the words facing the outside.
9. Poke a tiny hole in the top of the circle and add string for a hanger, or tape the string to the top of the circle and hang it in a window.
10. Look at the colorful circle to memorize the verse.

Circle Pattern

Apart from me you can do nothing.

John 15:5b

Acts 1:8

"'But you will receive power when the Holy Spirit comes on you; and you will be my witnesses in Jerusalem and in all Judea and Samaria, and to the ends of the earth.'"

Materials

- pattern (below)
- white paper
- 2 paper plates
- crayons or colored markers
- scissors
- hole punch
- colored yarn

Finished Product

Directions

1. Copy the pattern onto white paper.
2. Color and cut out the pattern.
3. Cut one of the paper plates in half.
4. Color the paper plates (the whole one and the half).
5. Hold the paper plates on top of each other, front to front, and punch holes around the edges of both.
6. Sew yarn in and out of the holes to attach the half plate to the bottom of the other plate, front to front, to make a basket. Tie at ends.
7. Glue the Bible verse pattern to the paper plate basket.
8. If you want to be a witness for Jesus, write the names of unsaved friends on slips of paper and put them in the basket. Take one out each day. Pray for that person and look for a chance to tell him or her about Jesus.

Verse Pattern

"But you will receive power when the Holy Spirit comes on you; and you will be my witnesses in Jerusalem, and in all Judea and Samaria, and to the ends of the earth." (Acts 1:8)

Acts 4:12

"'Salvation is found in no one else, for there is no other name under heaven given to men by which we must be saved.'"

Materials

- pattern (page 100)
- paper
- crayons or colored markers
- scissors
- glue

Directions

1. Copy the Bible verse pattern and cut it out.
2. Color the picture.
3. Carefully cut out the letters of the word JESUS on the Bible verse sheet.
4. Color a plain sheet of paper with bright rainbow colors. Cover the whole sheet.
5. Glue the Bible verse sheet on top of the sheet you colored with rainbow colors.
6. Look at the rainbow colors showing through Jesus' name.
7. Memorize the Bible verse.

Finished Product

"Salvation is found in no one else, for there is no other name under heaven given to men by which we must be saved." (Acts 4:12)

Acts 16:31a

"'. . . Believe in the Lord Jesus and you will be saved.'"

Materials

- patterns (below)
- scissors
- 2 paper or Styrofoam™ saucers
- crayons or colored markers
- red yarn
- glue
- hole punch
- white paper

Directions

1. Copy the Bible verse patterns onto white paper and cut them out.
2. Cut the center out of the saucers.
3. Glue the saucer rims together, front to front.
4. Wrap red yarn around the saucer rim in four places with equal distances between them.
5. Glue or tie the ends of the yarn at the back of the saucers to secure them.
6. Glue the Bible verse words on the saucer as shown.
7. Punch a small hole in the top of the "lifesaver" and attach yarn to hang.

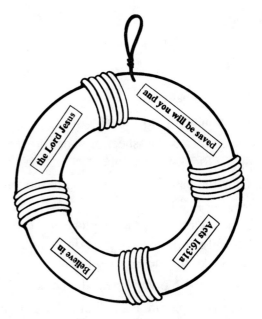

Finished Product

Verse Patterns

"Believe in

the Lord Jesus

and you will be saved."

Acts 16:31a

Romans 3:23

"For all have sinned and fall short of the glory of God."

Materials

- patterns (below)
- crayons or colored markers
- scissors
- glitter
- paper
- glue

Directions

1. Copy the patterns.
2. Color and cut out the patterns.
3. On an 8½" x 11" sheet of paper draw a mountain scene with a space for sky at the top.
4. Glue the pattern of the person in the left hand bottom 4" space of your picture.
5. Glue the cloud of God's glory at the very top of your picture. Spread a thin layer of glue on the cloud and sprinkle glitter on it. Shake off the excess glitter.
6. Glue the Bible verse near the person.
7. Fold your picture back about 5" from the bottom (just above the person). Then fold it down about 4" from the top. You should be able to see everything but 1" of your picture with the person almost touching God's glory cloud.
8. Read the Bible verse and unfold the picture to see how far people really are from reaching God's glory.

Finished Product

For all have sinned and fall short of the glory of God. (Romans 3:23)

GOD'S GLORY

Romans 5:8

"But God demonstrates his own love for us in this:
While we were still sinners, Christ died for us."

Materials

- pattern (page 104)
- cardstock
- tissue paper (various colors)
- crayons or colored markers
- clear adhesive plastic
- scissors
- glue
- hole punch
- string or thread

Directions

1. Copy the pattern on cardstock.

2. Cut out the pattern. Carefully cut out the inner "window" portions of the pattern.

3. Cut pieces of colored tissue paper to fit the cut-out portions. Glue the tissue paper on to make it look like a stained glass window.

4. Carefully cover the front and back of the window with clear adhesive plastic to protect it. Cut off the excess.

5. Punch a hole in the top of the window and tie a piece of string or thread on it.

6. Hang the stained glass window in a real window so the sun can shine through the colored parts.

7. Every time you look at the window, read the Bible verse and remember what Jesus did for you.

Finished Product

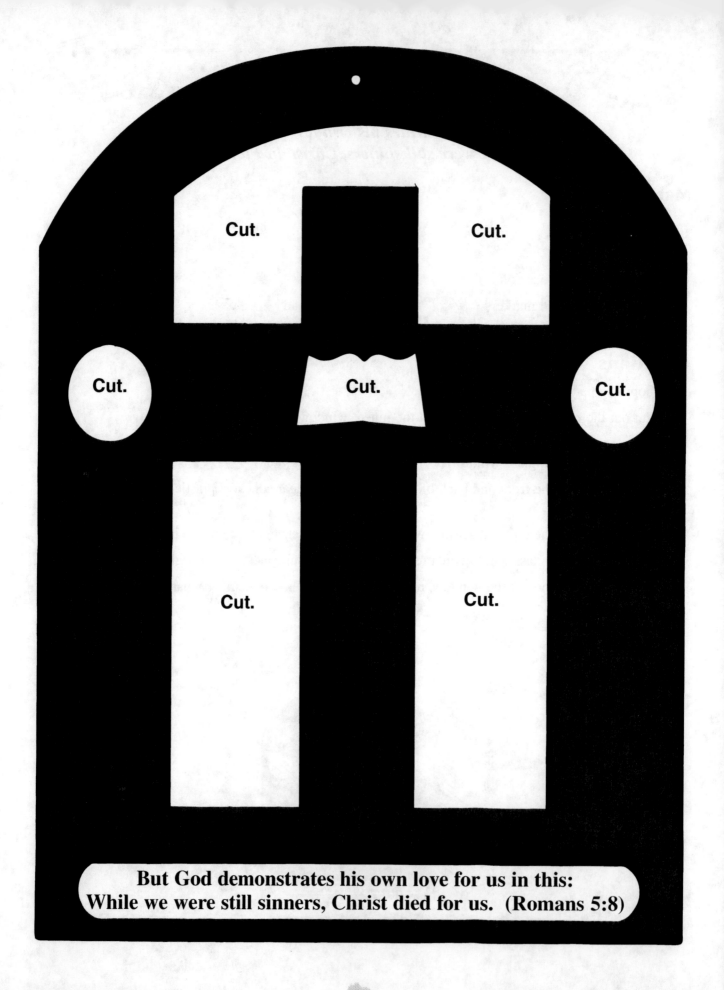

But God demonstrates his own love for us in this:
While we were still sinners, Christ died for us. (Romans 5:8)

"For the wages of sin is death, but the gift of God is eternal life in Christ Jesus our Lord."

Materials

- pattern (below)
- scissors
- cardstock
- crayons or colored markers

Directions

1. Copy the Bible pattern on cardstock.
2. Color the pattern and cut it out.
3. Fold the pattern on the dashed lines so the Bible verse reference is on the top, the first part of the verse is in the middle and the last part of the verse is at the bottom.
4. Memorize the Bible verse by unfolding the product.
5. Keep the fold-up art project in your pocket or in your Bible as a tool for telling friends about Jesus.

Finished Product

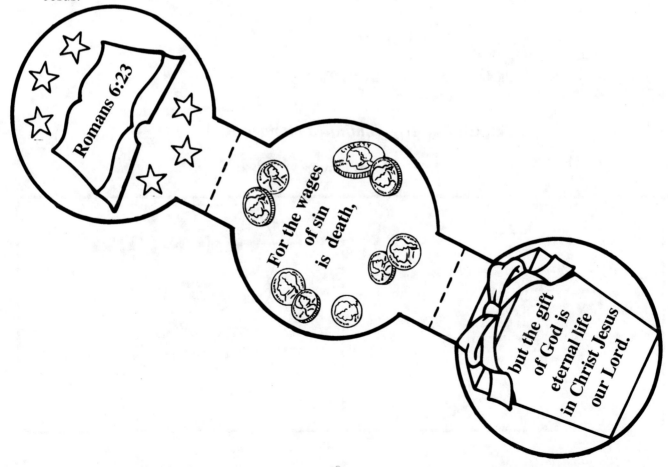

Romans 6:23

For the wages of sin is death,

but the gift of God is eternal life in Christ Jesus our Lord.

Romans 8:38–39

"For I am convinced that neither death nor life, neither angels nor demons, neither the present nor the future, nor any powers, neither height nor depth, nor anything else in all creation, will be able to separate us from the love of God that is in Christ Jesus our Lord."

Materials

- book pattern (below and on page 107)
- scissors
- cardstock
- crayons or colored markers

Directions

1. Copy the book pattern below and on page 107 onto cardstock.
2. Color the pictures and write your name on the front cover.
3. Cut apart the pages on page 107 and stack them in numbered order.
4. Cut out the front cover (below). Fold the cover on the dashed line.
5. Put the numbered pages inside the folded cover and staple them together on the left side.
6. Read the words in the booklet to memorize the Bible verses.

Finished Product

Book Pattern *(continued on page 107)*

Front Cover

For I am convinced that neither death nor life,

1

neither angels nor demons,

2

neither the present nor the future,

3

nor any powers,

4

neither height nor depth,

5

nor anything else in all creation,

6

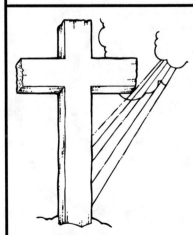

will be able to separate us from the love of God that is in Christ Jesus our Lord.

7

Romans 8:38–39

8

1 Corinthians 10:31

*"So whether you eat or drink or whatever you do,
do it all for the glory of God."*

Materials

- patterns (this page and page 109)
- 11" x 17" construction paper or colored cardstock
- white paper
- crayons or colored markers
- scissors
- glue
- fine glitter
- clear adhesive plastic

Finished Product

Directions

1. Copy the patterns onto white paper.

2. Color and cut out the patterns.

3. Glue the patterns on an 11" x 17" sheet of construction paper or cardstock.

4. Use crayons, markers, glue, and glitter to make your own designs on the sheet. Allow to dry.

5. Carefully cover both sides of the sheet with clear adhesive plastic for a durable place mat.

6. Every time you use your place mat, read the Bible verse and remember that God cares about everything you do, even your eating and drinking.

Patterns

So whether you eat or drink or whatever you do, do it all for the glory of God. (1 Corinthians 10:31)

Dear Father,
Thank You for the
good things You give me
to eat and drink.

Galatians 2:20

"'I have been crucified with Christ and I no longer live, but Christ lives in me.
The life I live in the body, I live by faith in the Son of God
who loved me and gave himself for me.'"

Materials

- patterns (below)
- scissors
- cardstock
- crayons or colored markers
- hole punch
- metal clasp ring (or colored yarn)

Finished Product

Directions

1. Copy the Bible verse patterns on cardstock.
2. Decorate each Bible verse card with your own drawings and designs.
3. Cut the cards apart.
4. Punch a hole in the top left side of each card.
5. Put the cards in order on a metal ring (or tie them together with yarn).
6. Go through the cards every day until you have the Bible verse memorized.

Verse Card Patterns

"I have been crucified with Christ	and I no longer live,	but Christ lives in me.	The life I live in the body,
I live by faith in the Son of God,	who loved me	and gave himself for me."	Galatians 2:20

Galatians 5:22–23a

"But the fruit of the Spirit is love, joy, peace, patience, kindness, goodness, faithfulness, gentleness and self control."

Materials

- patterns (this page and page 112)
- scissors
- cardstock
- crayons or colored markers
- heavy cardboard (at least 6" x 8")
- glue
- small envelope

Directions

1. Copy the patterns on cardstock.
2. Color and cut out the patterns.
3. Glue the grape cluster on a thick piece of cardboard.
4. Say the Bible verses. As you name each fruit of the Spirit, put the matching grape on the numbered spot in the grape cluster.
5. Keep the grapes in an envelope glued to the back of the grape cluster.
6. Put the grape puzzle together often to memorize the Bible verse.

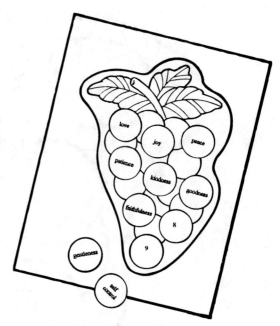

Finished Product

Grape Patterns

love 1	joy 2	peace 3	patience 4	kindness 5
goodness 6	faithfulness 7	gentleness 8	self-control 9	

Cluster Pattern

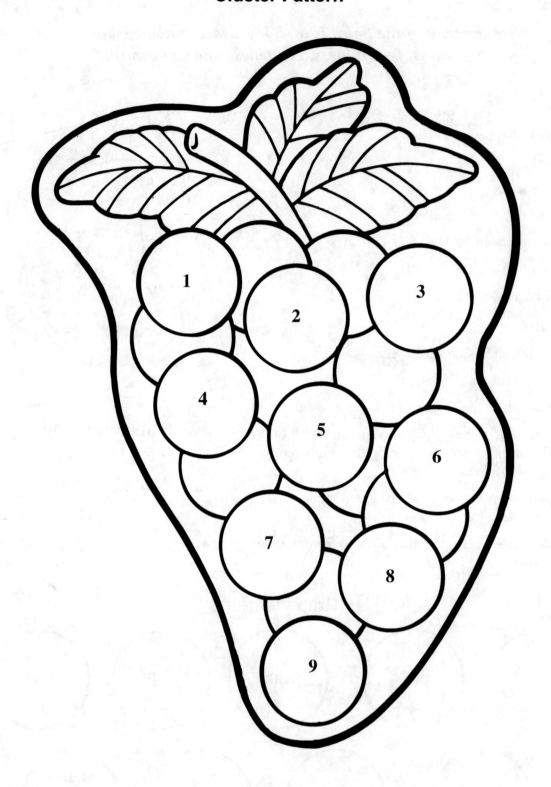

Ephesians 2:8

*"For it is by grace you have been saved, through faith—
and this not from yourselves, it is the gift of God."*

Materials

- patterns (below)
- cardstock
- crayons or colored markers
- ribbon (or small gift bow)
- tape
- scissors

Directions

1. Copy the patterns on cardstock.
2. Color and cut out the patterns.
3. Fold the box pattern on the dashed lines.
4. Tape the sides of the box together.
5. Tie ribbon into a bow and tape it to the box lid (or attach a gift bow to the lid).
6. Fold the Bible verse card and place it in the gift box. Take it out to memorize it.

Finished Product

Box Pattern

To: You
From: God

A gift
for you!

Verse Pattern

For it is by grace you have been saved, through faith—and this not from yourselves, it is the gift of God. (Ephesians 2:8)

Ephesians 4:32

"Be kind and compassionate to one another,
forgiving each other, just as in Christ God forgave you."

Materials

- patterns (below)
- cardstock
- crayons or colored markers
- craft sticks
- glue
- scissors
- paper or Styrofoam™ cup

Directions

1. Copy the patterns on cardstock.
2. Color and cut out the flower patterns.
3. Glue each flower to a craft stick for a stem. (Color the craft sticks green if you want.)
4. Decorate the cup with crayons or markers.
5. Write the Bible verse reference, Ephesians 4:32, in big letters on the cup.
6. Put the flowers in the cup for a kindness bouquet.
7. Take the flowers out of the cup and try to line them up in correct order to show the Bible verse.
8. Memorize the verse by arranging the flowers until you can do it quickly without looking in your Bible.

Finished Product

Be kind

and compassionate

Flower Patterns

to one another,

forgiving each other,

just as in Christ

God forgave you.

Ephesians 6:10–11

*"Finally, be strong in the Lord and in his mighty power.
Put on the full armor of God so that you can take your stand
against the devil's schemes."*

Materials

- patterns (this page and page 116)
- cardstock
- scissors
- cardboard
- tape
- hole punch
- string or fishing line
- crayons or colored markers

Directions

1. Copy the patterns on cardstock.
2. Color and cut out the patterns.
3. Cut out a piece of cardboard about 6" x 11".
4. Draw an open Bible on both sides of the cardboard and color it.
5. Tape string or fishing line of various lengths to the Bible verse patterns.
6. Tape the other ends of the string to the bottom of the cardboard open Bible to make a mobile.
7. Punch three holes in the top of the cardboard and attach string or fishing line for a hanger.
8. Read the Bible verse in numbered order from the armor shapes.

Sword Pattern

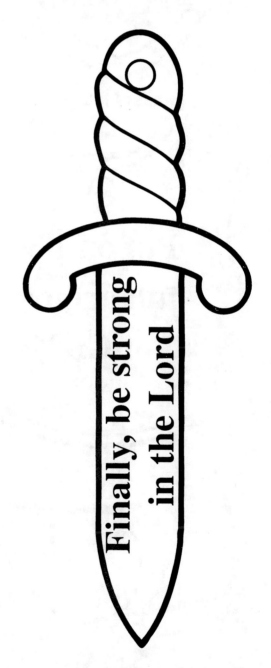

Finally, be strong in the Lord

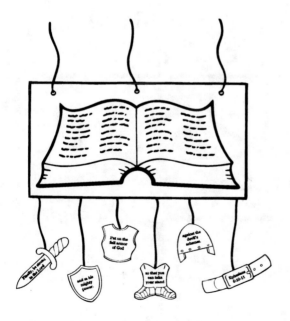

Finished Product

Shield Pattern

Boots Pattern

and in his mighty power.

so that you can take your stand

Breast Plate Pattern

Helmet Pattern

Put on the full armor of God

against the devil's schemes.

Belt Pattern

Ephesians 6:10–11

Philippians 2:14

"Do everything without complaining or arguing."

Materials

- pattern (below)
- scissors
- cardstock
- crayons or colored markers
- clear adhesive plastic
- magnetic strip
- glue

Directions

1. Copy the pattern on cardstock.
2. Color and cut out the pattern.
3. Cover the pattern, front and back, with clear adhesive plastic. Trim off the excess plastic.
4. Glue a piece of magnetic strip to the back of the flower and keep it on your family refrigerator.
5. Challenge your family to memorize the Bible verse with you (and do what it says).

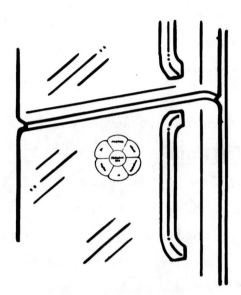

Finished Product

Flower Pattern

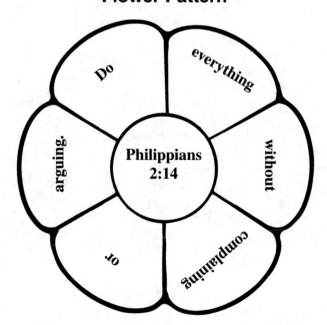

Philippians 4:4

"Rejoice in the Lord always. I will say it again: Rejoice!"

Materials

- pattern (page 119)
- cardstock
- string or yarn
- crayons or colored markers

- scissors
- glue
- glitter
- hole punch

Directions

1. Copy the pattern on cardstock.
2. Color the pattern and cut it out.
3. Trace a layer of glue over the "Rejoice" letters and sprinkle glitter on them. Shake off the excess.
4. Punch holes in the top of the pattern (one on the right and one the left).
5. Tie string or yarn in the holes.
6. Then hang the Bible verse in a window as a reminder to rejoice!

in the Lord always. I will say it again:
Rejoice! (Philippians 4:4)

Finished Product

Rejoice

in the Lord always. I will say it again: Rejoice! (Philippians 4:4)

Philippians 4:6

"Do not be anxious about anything, but in everything, by prayer and petition, with thanksgiving, present your requests to God."

Materials

- pattern (below)
- scissors
- cardstock
- crayons or colored markers
- tape

Directions

1. Copy the pattern on cardstock.

2. Color and cut out the pattern.

3. Fold the pattern on the dashed lines and tape the ends together to stand it up.

4. Keep the prayer reminder near your bed to help you remember to begin and end each day with prayer. God wants you to talk to Him often.

Finished Product

Prayer Pattern

Do not be anxious about anything, but in everything, by prayer and petition, with thanksgiving, present your requests to God.
(Philippians 4:6)

Philippians 4:13

"I can do everything through him who gives me strength."

Materials

- pattern (below)
- scissors
- cardstock
- crayons or colored markers
- tape

Finished Product

Directions

1. Copy the pattern on cardstock.
2. Color and cut out the pattern. Sign your name on the line marked "name."
3. Fold the pattern on the dashed lines and tape the ends together to make it stand up.
4. Place your name plate on your desk.
5. Memorize the Bible verse as a reminder that God will help you do anything He wants you to do.

Name Plate Pattern

(name)

☆ ★ ☆ ★ ☆ ★ ☆ ★

☆ ☆ ☆ ☆ ☆ ☆ ☆

I can do everything through him who gives me strength. (Philippians 4:13)

Colossians 3:20

"Children, obey your parents in everything, for this pleases the Lord."

Materials

- pattern (below)
- scissors
- cardstock
- crayons or colored markers
- glue
- paper
- photograph of family
- 4 craft sticks
- decorative stickers
- yarn or ribbon (or magnetic tape)

Directions

1. Glue the four craft sticks in a square for a picture frame.

2. Copy the Bible verse pattern and cut it out.

3. Glue the verse on the bottom of the frame.

4. Decorate the rest of the frame with designs and decorative stickers.

5. Cut out a piece of cardstock a little larger than the hole in the middle of the frame.

6. Glue the cardstock to the back of the frame on the bottom and two sides.

7. Glue yarn or ribbon to the back of the frame for a hanger. (Or glue a magnetic strip on the back so you can keep it on your family refrigerator.)

8. Slip a photograph of you and your parents in the frame.

9. Memorize the Bible verse on the frame and say it to your parents.

Finished Product

Verse Pattern

Children, obey your parents in everything, for this pleases the Lord. (Colossians 3:20)

Colossians 3:23

"Whatever you do, work at it with all your heart,
as working for the Lord, not for men."

Materials

- patterns (below)
- metal key ring
- clear adhesive plastic
- crayons or colored markers
- scissors
- hole punch
- cardstock
- glue

Finished Product

Directions

1. Make one copy of the beaver pattern and one copy of the Bible verse pattern on cardstock.
2. Color the beaver pattern and the Bible verse pattern.
3. Cut out the patterns.
4. Punch a hole in the top of each pattern at the same spot.
5. Glue the patterns together, carefully lining them up so the holes match. The colored beaver pattern should be on the top and the Bible verse on the back.
6. After the glue dries, cover the patterns, front and back, with clear adhesive plastic to protect them. Cut around the patterns, leaving a plastic border of about half an inch.
7. Insert a metal ring in the hole and add your keys.
8. Look at the Bible verse often to memorize it and to practice what it says.

Beaver Pattern

Verse Pattern

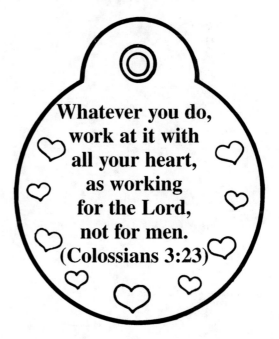

Whatever you do,
work at it with
all your heart,
as working
for the Lord,
not for men.
(Colossians 3:23)

1 Timothy 4:12

"Don't let anyone look down on you because you are young, but set an example for the believers in speech, in life, in love, in faith and in purity."

Materials

- pattern (page 125)
- scissors
- cardstock
- crayons or colored markers
- clear adhesive plastic

Directions

1. Copy the pattern on cardstock.

2. Color and cut out the pattern, including the center hole.

3. Draw a picture or write what you want on the other side of the pattern.

4. Cover both sides of the pattern with clear adhesive plastic to protect it and cut off excess from edges and center hole.

5. Hang it on the doorknob of your room at home. If the doorknob will not fit through the center hole, cut a few slits around its edge.

6. Memorize the Bible verse and try to do what it says.

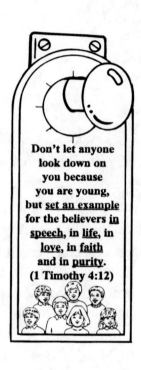

Finished Product

Doorknob Hanger Pattern

Cut out.

Don't let anyone look down on you because you are young, but <u>set an example</u> for the believers <u>in</u> <u>speech</u>, in <u>life</u>, in love, in <u>faith</u> and in <u>purity</u>. (1 Timothy 4:12)

2 Timothy 3:16

"All Scripture is God-breathed and is useful for teaching, rebuking, correcting and training in righteousness."

Materials

- pattern (page 127)
- colored cardstock
- clear adhesive plastic *(optional)*

- scissors
- business envelope
- pencil

Directions

1. Copy the Bible pattern on colored cardstock. (*Optional:* Cover the pattern, front and back, with clear adhesive plastic.)

2. Cut the Bible pattern into puzzle pieces as marked.

3. Lay the puzzle pieces out in scrambled order.

4. Try to put the Bible puzzle together.

5. When you are finished, read the Bible verse.

6. Put the puzzle together several times, trying to do it faster each time. Be sure to read the Bible verse each time to memorize it.

7. Keep the puzzle pieces in an envelope. Print the Bible verse reference, 2 Timothy 3:16, on the back of the envelope.

Finished Product

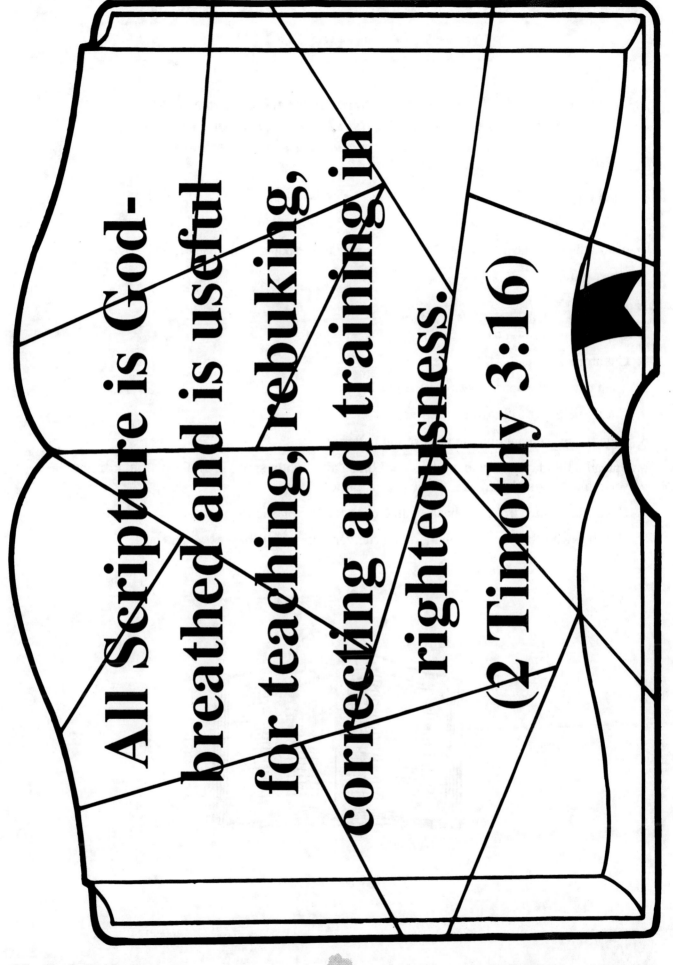

All Scripture is God-breathed and is useful for teaching, rebuking, correcting and training in righteousness. (2 Timothy 3:16)

Hebrews 4:12

"For the word of God is living and active. Sharper than any double-edged sword, it penetrates even to dividing soul and spirit, joints and marrow; it judges the thoughts and attitudes of the heart."

Materials

- pattern (page 129)
- cardstock
- clear adhesive plastic
- silver glitter
- scissors
- glue
- tissue paper (various colors)

Directions

1. Copy the pattern on cardstock.

2. Cut around the pattern.

3. Then cut out the spaces between the black sections.

4. Cut tissue paper to fit over the spaces.

5. Glue the tissue paper on the back of the pattern.

6. Spread a thin layer of glue on the sword blade and lightly sprinkle glitter over it, keeping the verse mostly visible. Shake off the excess glitter.

7. Cover the sword, front and back, with clear adhesive plastic to protect it. Trim excess.

8. Use the sword bookmark to mark a favorite verse in your Bible.

Finished Product

Bookmark Pattern

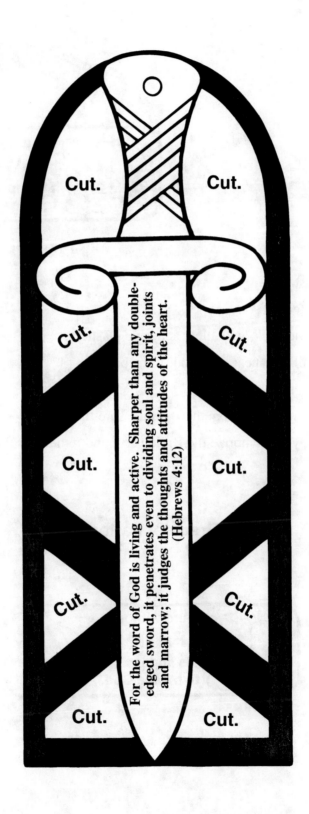

Cut.   Cut.

Cut.   Cut.

Cut.   Cut.

Cut.   Cut.

Cut.   Cut.

For the word of God is living and active. Sharper than any double-edged sword, it penetrates even to dividing soul and spirit, joints and marrow; it judges the thoughts and attitudes of the heart. (Hebrews 4:12)

Hebrews 11:6a

"And without faith it is impossible to please God."

Materials

- pattern (below)
- scissors
- clear adhesive plastic
- cardstock
- crayons or colored markers
- gold cord or thin yarn
- nail

Finished Product

Directions

1. Copy the pattern on cardstock.
2. Color and cut out the pattern.
3. Cover the pattern, front and back, with clear adhesive plastic.
4. Use a nail to make a small hole near each end of the pattern.
5. Tie gold cord or thin yarn in each hole.
6. Tie the two ends of the cord or yarn together. (Make sure the bracelet will slip over your hand.)
7. Wear the bracelet to help you memorize the Bible verse and remember the importance of faith.

Bracelet Pattern

Hebrews 12:1

"Therefore, since we are surrounded by such a great cloud of witnesses, let us throw off everything that hinders and the sin that so easily entangles, and let us run with perseverance the race marked out for us."

Materials

- patterns (this page and page 132)
- scissors
- cardstock
- crayons or colored markers
- hole punch
- brad fastener

Finished Product

Directions

1. Copy the patterns on cardstock.

2. Color and cut out the patterns.

3. Punch a hole at the top of each of the legs and at the middle of the boy in the picture.

4. Use a brad fastener to attach the two legs to the boy at the back of the picture.

5. As you read the Bible verse, move the boy's legs to make him "run the race."

Leg Patterns

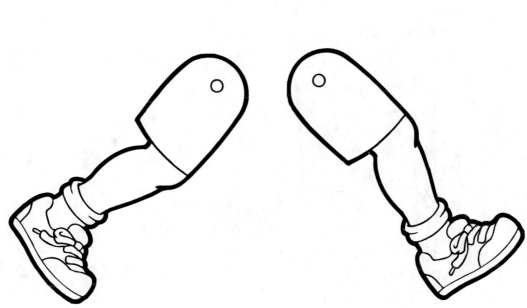

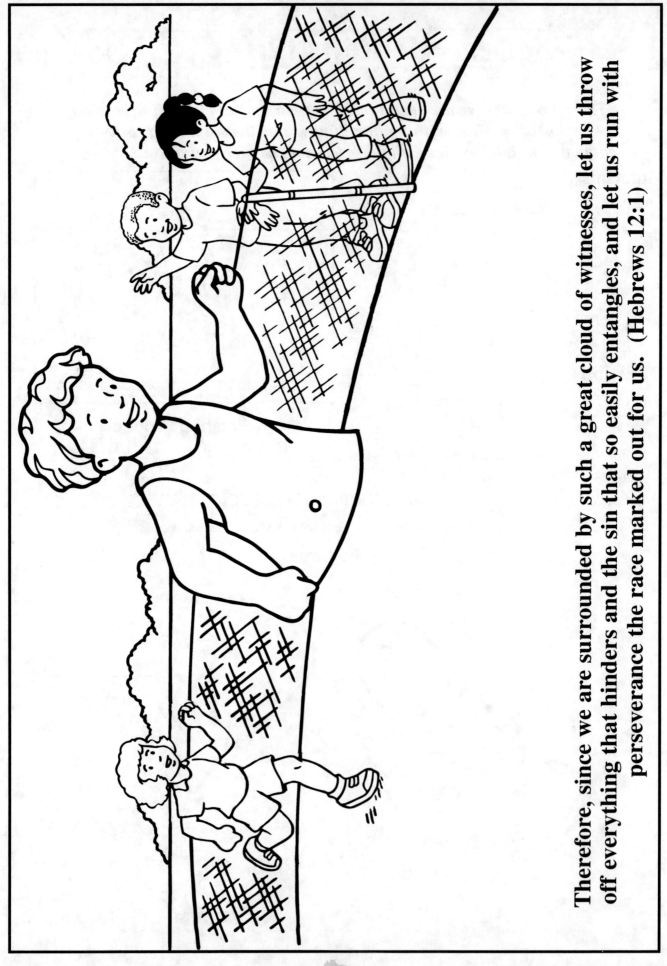

Therefore, since we are surrounded by such a great cloud of witnesses, let us throw off everything that hinders and the sin that so easily entangles, and let us run with perseverance the race marked out for us. (Hebrews 12:1)

132

Hebrews 13:5

"Keep your lives free from the love of money and be content with what you have, because God has said, 'Never will I leave you; never will I forsake you.'"

Materials

- patterns (below)
- scissors
- clear adhesive plastic
- green paper
- glue
- pencil

Finished Product

Directions

1. Copy the patterns on green paper.
2. Cut out the patterns. Sign your name on one line. Have a friend sign on the other line.
3. Glue the patterns back to back to make a five-dollar bill.
4. Cover the bill, front and back, with clear adhesive plastic.
5. Keep the money in your pocket, Bible, or wallet to help you memorize the Bible verse.

Money Patterns

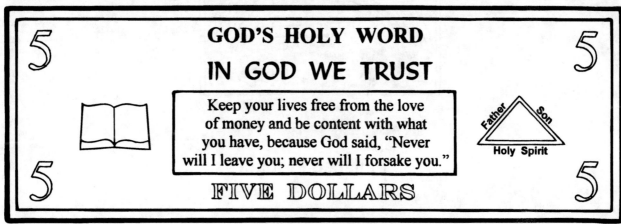

Hebrews 13:6

"So we say with confidence, 'The Lord is my helper;
I will not be afraid. What can man do to me?'"

Materials

- pattern (page 135)
- cardstock
- crayons or colored markers
- thick yarn (red, orange, yellow, green, blue, dark blue, violet)
- scissors
- glue
- cotton balls

Directions

1. Copy the pattern on cardstock.

2. Color and cut out the pattern. (Do not color the rainbow.)

3. Glue colored yarn on the rainbow, beginning with red at the top and ending with violet on the bottom.

4. Glue yellow yarn on the sun and cotton on the clouds.

5. Glue yarn around the picture for a frame.

6. Look at the picture to memorize the Bible verse.

Finished Product

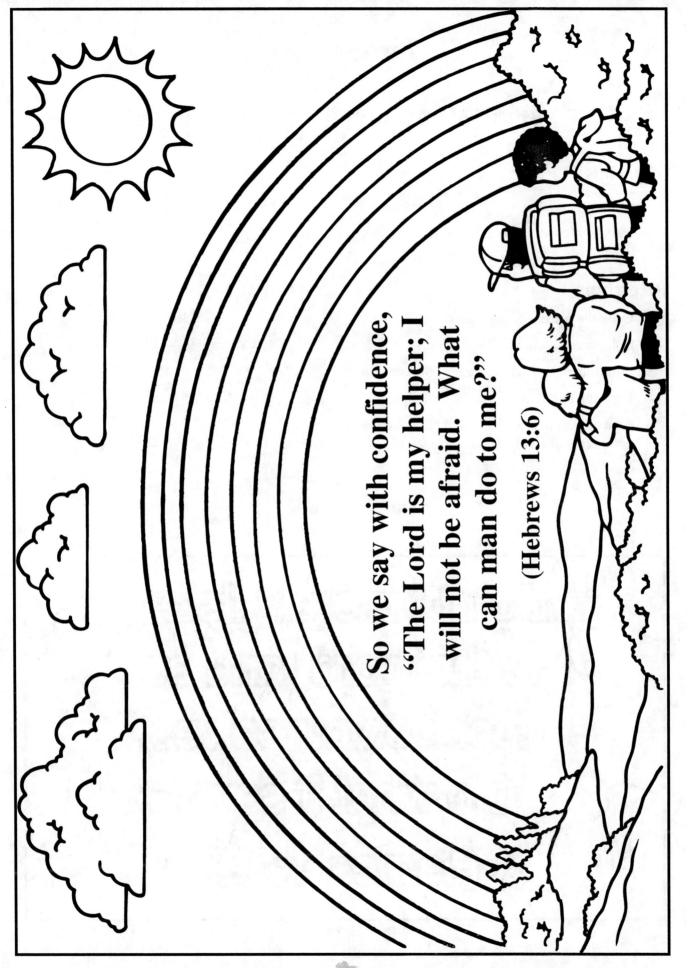

So we say with confidence,
"The Lord is my helper; I
will not be afraid. What
can man do to me?"
(Hebrews 13:6)

James 1:22

*"Do not merely listen to the word, and so deceive yourselves.
Do what it says."*

Materials

- pattern (below)
- cardstock
- colored markers or crayons
- scissors
- envelope
- pencil

Directions

1. Copy the pattern on cardstock.
2. Color and cut out the puzzle pieces.
3. Print James 1:22 on the back of the envelope.
4. Keep the puzzle pieces in the envelope.
5. Take out the puzzle pieces and put them together as you memorize the Bible verse.

Finished Product

Puzzle Pattern

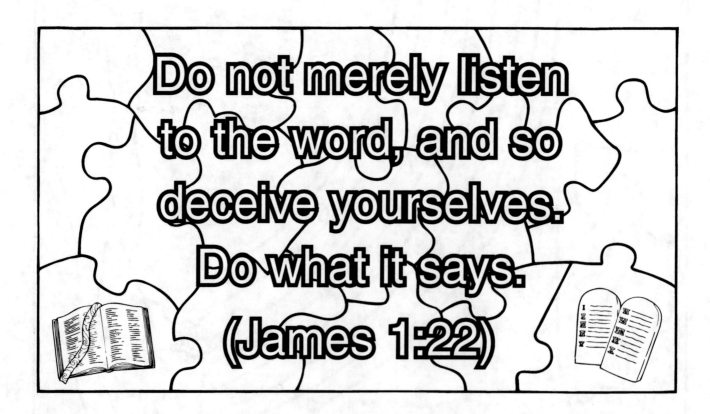

*"Submit yourselves, then, to God. Resist the devil,
and he will flee from you."*

Materials

- pattern (below)
- colored markers or crayons
- scissors
- paper

Directions

1. Copy the pattern.
2. Color and cut out the pattern.
3. Fold the pattern on the dashed lines to make a four-page booklet.
4. Read each part of the Bible verse and follow the directions on each page.
5. Use the booklet to memorize the Bible verse.

Finished Product

Book Pattern

Submit yourselves, then, to God. Explain what it means to "submit" to God. _____ _____ 2	**Resist the devil,** How does God help you resist the devil? _____ _____ 3
1 ʇ:ㄣ sǝɯɐſ	4 Draw a picture of yourself on the front of this booklet to show how you feel when you submit to God and resist the devil. and he will flee from you.

1 Peter 5:7

"Cast all your anxiety on him because he cares for you."

Materials

- patterns (below)
- colored markers or crayons
- string (two 4" pieces)
- hole punch
- scissors
- cardstock
- glue

Directions

1. Copy the patterns on cardstock.

2. Color and cut out the patterns.

3. Glue the two patterns together back to back, one right side up, the other upside down.

4. Use a hole punch to punch a hole on the right side of the circle and one on the left.

5. Tie a piece of string in one hole, then tie a piece of string in the other hole.

6. Hold the circle strings in each hand and twist the string between your thumb and first fingers. Then pull the strings taut to make the circle spin and see where your cares should go.

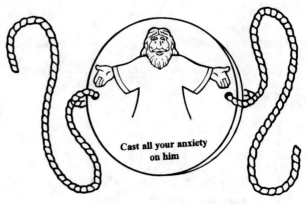

Finished Product

Circle Patterns

Cast all your anxiety
on him

MY
CARES

because he cares for
you. (1 Peter 5:7)

1 Peter 5:8

"Be self-controlled and alert. Your enemy the devil prowls around like a roaring lion looking for someone to devour."

Materials

- patterns (below)
- colored markers or crayons
- brown and yellow yarn
- tongue depressor
- scissors
- cardstock
- glue

Directions

1. Copy the lion and verse patterns on cardstock.

2. Color the lion pattern and cut it out.

3. Cut small lengths of brown and yellow yarn and glue them on the lion's mane.

4. Glue the lion on the end of a tongue depressor to make a stick puppet.

5. Carefully glue the Bible verse on the tongue depressor.

6. Hold up the lion as you say the Bible verse. Make the lion roar. Remember that the devil is even more dangerous than a hungry lion!

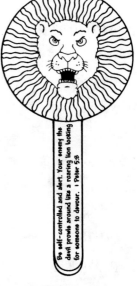

Finished Product

Lion Pattern

Verse Pattern

Be self-controlled and alert. Your enemy the devil prowls around like a roaring lion looking for someone to devour. 1 Peter 5:8

"If we confess our sins, he is faithful and just and will forgive us our sins and purify us from all unrighteousness."

Materials

- patterns (page 141)
- scissors
- cardstock
- crayons or colored markers
- glue
- ribbon or string
- 26" long strip of wide ribbon, construction paper, or crépe paper

Directions

1. Copy the letter patterns on cardstock.

2. Color the patterns and cut them out.

3. Space the letters evenly down the paper or ribbon strip.

4. Glue the letters onto the strip.

5. Glue a piece of ribbon or string to the top of the strip for a hanger.

6. Hang the word where you will see it often and memorize the Bible verse on the letters.

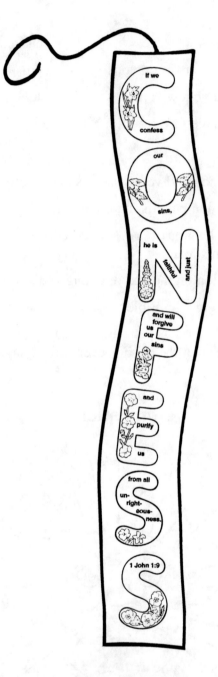

Finished Product

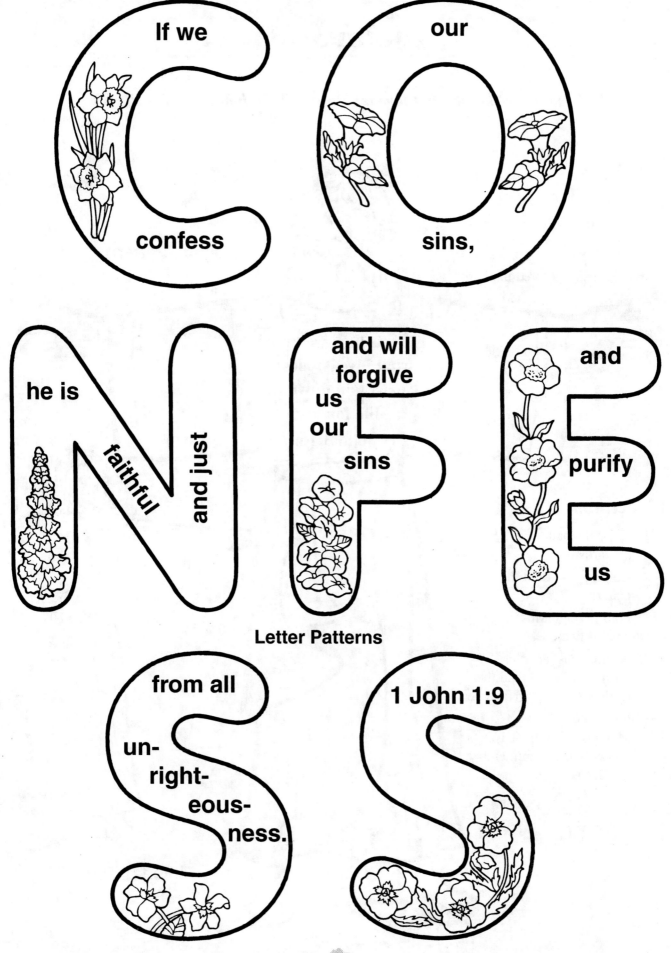

If we

our

confess

sins,

he is

and will
forgive
us
our
sins

and

faithful

and just

purify

us

Letter Patterns

from all

1 John 1:9

un-
right-
eous-
ness.

"This is how we know what love is: Jesus Christ laid down his life for us."

Materials

- pattern (on this page)
- scissors
- cardstock
- crayons or colored markers

Jesus Pattern

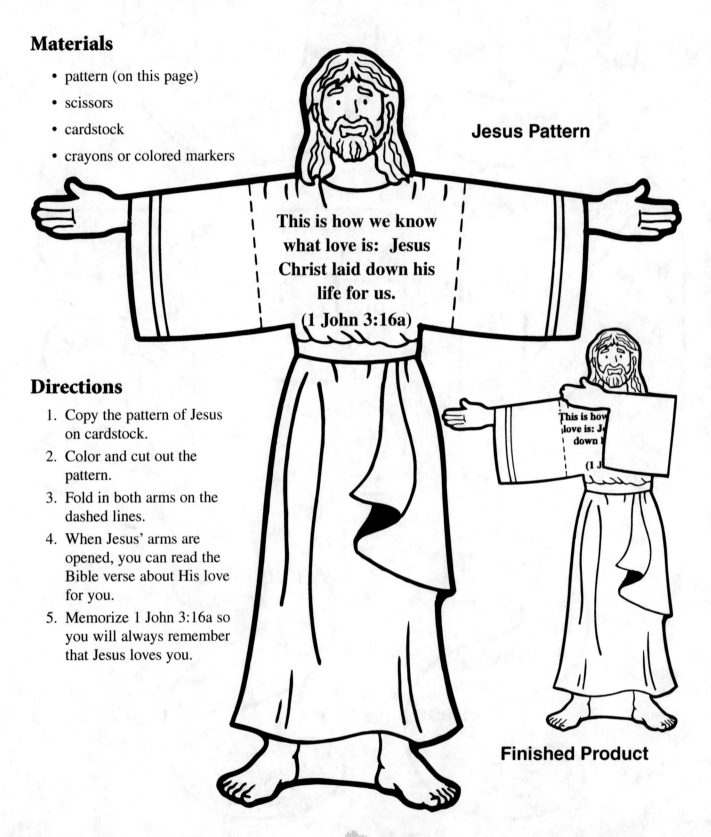

This is how we know what love is: Jesus Christ laid down his life for us.
(1 John 3:16a)

Directions

1. Copy the pattern of Jesus on cardstock.
2. Color and cut out the pattern.
3. Fold in both arms on the dashed lines.
4. When Jesus' arms are opened, you can read the Bible verse about His love for you.
5. Memorize 1 John 3:16a so you will always remember that Jesus loves you.

Finished Product

1 John 4:4

"You, dear children, are from God and have overcome them, because the one who is in you is greater than the one who is in the world."

Materials

Finished Product

- patterns (below)
- colored markers or crayons
- carbon paper
- paper plate
- scissors
- paper
- glue
- pen/pencil

Directions

1. Copy the patterns and cut them out.
2. Draw a line on the paper plate to divide it in half.
3. Place the Jesus pattern with carbon paper under it on the line on the plate.
4. Trace the Jesus pattern onto the paper plate.
5. Color the figure of Jesus. Color the rest of the plate to look like the earth.
6. Carefully cut around the figure of Jesus, leaving the bottom attached to the plate. Do not cut the top half off the plate; leave it attached.
7. Fold the plate in half so the figure of Jesus stands up.
8. Glue the Bible verse pattern on the front of the plate.

Jesus Pattern

Verse Pattern

You, dear children, are from God and have overcome them, because the one who is in you is greater than the one who is in the world. (1 John 4:4)

1 John 4:10

"This is love: not that we loved God, but that he loved us and sent his Son as an atoning sacrifice for our sins."

Materials

- pattern (on this page)
- scissors
- cardstock
- crayons or colored markers

Directions

1. Copy the cross pattern on cardstock.
2. Color and cut out the cross.
3. Fold the cross on the dashed lines this way:

    section 7 up to cover 6

    section 6 up to cover 5

    section 5 to the back

    section 4 to the left to cover 3

    section 2 to the right to cover 3 and 4

    section 1 back to cover 5, 6, and 7.

4. Unfold the cross in the numbered order of the sections and read the Bible verse.

1 John 4:10
1

This is love:
2

not that we loved God,
3

but that he loved us
4

and sent his Son
5

as an atoning sacrifice
6

for our sins.
7

Finished Product